Smart Girl's GUIDE.

TO GOING

VEGETARIAN

How to Look GREAT, Feel FABULOUS, and Be a BETTER YOU

RACHEL MELTZER WARREN, MS, RDN

sourcebooks
fire

Published by Sourcebooks Fire, an imprint of Sourcebooks, Inc.
P.O. Box 4410, Naperville, Illinois 60567-4410
(630) 961-3900
Fax: (630) 961-2168
teenfire.sourcebooks.com

Library of Congress Cataloging-in-Publication data is on file with
the publisher.

Printed and bound in the United States of America.

VP 10 9 8 7 6 5 4 3 2 1

For Scott, who eats everything.

CONTENTS

• INTRODUCTION •

Dear Readers:

When I was twelve years old, I became a vegetarian. A cruddy one. A vegetarian who ate rice for dinner and thought it was perfectly OK to order french fries for lunch when my friends were getting burgers. As a result of my less-than-stellar food choices, I constantly battled low energy and had a handful of pounds to lose and a lot of frustration over constant questioning from adults about my eating habits.

I never really liked meat, to be honest—many of my early memories involve choking down some form of beef or chicken so I could justify eating the french fries (again, those fries!), tater tots, or baked potato that came with it. So that made it easy to entertain the idea of giving up meat entirely. But cutting it out of my diet didn't happen overnight.

The next thing that got me thinking about saying so long to meat was my affection for animals. I loved animals. Still do—just ask anyone who knows me how often I talk about my beagle Penny. As a young kid, I owned countless fish and gerbils. Many of my birthday parties were at science museums and environmental centers and involved petting rabbits, snakes, and other wildlife. As I got older, I started to put the pieces together— that chicken comes from, well, chicken. That steak is just a friendlier way of saying cow. I didn't like it one bit. That taste of meat that I already didn't love grew even worse in my mouth.

The final straw on my road to vegetarianism was as simple as this: my parents bought new leather couches. I was horrified. "You're going to make me sit on *a cow*?!," I exclaimed. "That's it!" my mother said. "I'm sick of this! You want to save the animals when it's good for you, but when you're in the mood for a hamburger, it all goes out the window!" She was right. I hated when my mother was right. But little did she know, I was never really all that into those burgers, anyway (I still really just wanted the fries!). "I'm never going to eat a hamburger again," I proclaimed.

My parents still have the leather couches. And I still haven't eaten a hamburger.

Since that middle school declaration, I've gone on to high school, to college to be a writer, and to graduate school to be a registered dietitian nutritionist (RDN). While it's been no shock that I've met a lot of other vegetarians along the way, one thing that surprised me is how many have a similar story to mine. Most all of the vegetarians I encounter stopped eating meat when they were somewhere around middle school or high school. And most of them, like me, played around with the idea of vegetarianism—going vegan and then adding back in dairy, giving up red meat first and then chicken and fish, for instance—before they settled on the degree that felt right to them (for the record, as an adult I started eating some fish, which I continue to do today). I've also met a lot of adults who mention that even though they eat meat now, they didn't for a couple of years during middle or high school.

In my work as a nutritionist, I cross paths with a lot of

teenagers who are what I like to call "veg-curious"—they're thinking about giving up meat, but aren't quite sure what their particular brand of vegetarianism is going to look like. Or they're confident about what type of vegetarian they want to be, but are struggling with how to do so healthfully or how to convince the adults in their life that this is a good idea. I'm always looking for books, websites, and other resources that I can recommend to my clients. But when I started looking for a place to send what I call my "VegHeads,"—the huge number of teens and preteens figuring out just how they fit into the world of vegetarianism—I fell flat. I found no book or website that encouraged teens to find the level of vegetarianism that worked for them and helped them do so without falling into the same traps that I did.

Which is why I'm writing this book. I know that deciding to be a vegetarian isn't always super clear-cut. You may decide to go veg and then wake up in a cold sweat because you ate chicken pot pie for dinner ("OMG, chicken! Argh!"). Or you may actively make the decision to stop eating just red meat for now and decide about everything else later on. According to what I've learned as I've been on this journey, becoming a vegetarian—for anyone, but especially for teenagers—is a process. Which is why you will often see me using terms other than "vegetarian" to describe us in this book. VegHead, flexitarian, veg-curious, vegetarian-in-training—any way you slice it, we're all just people who are thinking a lot about the way we eat, contemplating giving up meat or just eating less of it in a way that works for us, for the reasons we've decided are right for us. And while we're at it, we're going to learn to be healthy about it from the start. I'm going to make sure you're all set with tips on how to wow your friends and family with delish food, and answer questions about how to go through life not eating meat or more so you don't have to go through the same troubles I did.

In the first chapter of this book, you'll find a quiz that helps you determine where you are on the veg spectrum. Maybe you're just thinking about shifting to a *plant-based* diet...but you're not sure it's right for you. Perhaps you've been a vegan for a while now. Most likely, though, you're somewhere in between. Wherever you fall, the rest of the book will be about meeting you where YOU are, and giving you tips on getting the nutrients your body needs, standing up for yourself in social situations, how to eat out meat-free, and more that help you be the healthiest, most vibrant, energetic, and happiest VegHead you can be.

So, readers, congratulations on being the kind of person who takes what she eats so seriously. Wherever you end up going, it says a lot about you that you are taking a close look at the food you put in your body and what it means to you. This is a great opportunity to start taking care of yourself from the inside out. I'm so excited to be joining you for this ride.

Love and veggies,
Rachel

What the heck is...*plant-based*?

Generally, this refers to eating in a way that includes more plant foods—vegetables, fruits, beans, grains—and fewer animal foods like meat, eggs, and dairy. It doesn't mean you're a vegetarian, but rather that your diet is leaning in that direction.

. CHAPTER 1 .

HOW VEG IS YOUR HEAD?

THIS BOOK IS HERE TO SUPPORT
YOU, WHEREVER YOU ARE.

You may have opened this book knowing exactly what you want to accomplish, whether it's give up meat every once in a while or let go of it altogether. But for many of us, going veg is a work in progress. You may love the idea of being vegan, but for now simply going meat-free may suit your life a bit better. Or maybe you're just not sure. This quiz will help you determine what type of VegHead you are today. Remember, this is subject to change— Monday's meat-phobe may be Tuesday's chicken finger fan. That's OK. This book is here to support you, wherever you are.

The most important thing to keep in mind about this quiz is that it is just for fun. If the result you get is not at all what you had in mind, no worries. You know what brought you here and you will figure out where this journey is taking you in good time.

1. I currently eat meat:
a. All the time
b. Most of the time
c. Some of the time
d. Hardly ever
e. Never

2. Which of the following statements best describes your feelings toward being green and environmentally conscious?

a. I don't pay too much attention to recycling and conservation.

b. I want to help, but I'm not sure how much impact I can really have.

c. I recycle whenever I can and never leave the water running when I brush my teeth.

d. Green is my color! I compost, only drink water out of a reusable container, and buy all of my clothes secondhand from thrift shops.

3. When you eat out, how long does it take you to decide on what to order?

a. No time at all—I mostly always get the same thing!

b. Just a minute—I have my favorites that I usually rotate through.

c. A while—I like to try new things so I make sure to read the menu to see if there's anything interesting.

d. Longer than everyone else at the table...oh, and I sometimes change my mind after the order's been taken.

4. Which of the following foods would you be least likely to live without?

a. Burgers. Just gotta have one sometimes!

b. Chicken. It's a staple in my house!

c. Tuna. Isn't that what brown bag lunches are all about?

d. Ice cream! A life without ice cream is a life not worth living!

e. None of the above—I'd be just fine without any of these.

5. What city would you most like to eat in?

a. Dallas, TX—mmm, barbecue!

b. New York, NY—so many options on every corner!

c. New Orleans, LA—seafood central!

d. Boston, MA—the highest consumption of ice cream in the US!

e. Berkeley, CA—it's cool to be organic and everything is veg-friendly!

6. Which fictional character do you most associate with?

a. Wimpy from Popeye—he's almost always eating hamburgers.

b. Popeye himself—he loves spinach and holds the veggie responsible for his super strength.

c. Captain Planet—the superhero who defends the world from pollution and natural disasters.

d. Lisa Simpson—the politically active eight-year-old became a vegetarian when her mom served lamb chops for dinner the same day she bonded with a petting zoo lamb.

7. How do you feel about stopping at the grocery store with your parents?

a. Avoid at all costs.

b. It's OK because that way I have some say in what we eat at home.

c. I like it as long as it doesn't take too long.

d. Love it. I could go every day.

8. What's your idea of an amazing vacation?

a. Hawaii

b. Europe

c. Tahiti

d. India

9. What is your favorite flavor?

a. Savory—like meat, mushrooms, and parmesan cheese.

b. Salty

c. Sour

d. Sweet

10. Bottom line, what are your feelings on eating animal products (including meat, fish, dairy, eggs)?

a. I like them, but I want to eat them less.

b. They're OK, but I worry that if I gave them up I wouldn't know what to eat.

c. Nothing that has a face—but foods that don't hurt the living animal like milk and eggs don't bother me.

d. I think it's not cool and would like to avoid it altogether.

DETERMINE YOUR SCORE:
For every a: 1 point
For every b: 2 points
For every c: 3 points
For every d: 4 points
For every e: 5 points

If you scored 10–15, you are thinking about going veg, but you're not quite ready to take the leap—and that makes you

Veg-Curious. You totally get the idea of giving up meat alto-gether, but you also like a good burger every now and then. Also, you're somewhat set in your ways and not looking to mix things up too much. By making just some of your meals plant-based, you can dip your toe in the water of meatlessness—and give a little boost to your health and the well-being of the planet. You may want to start by adopting the Meatless Monday program—begin each week with a day's worth of VegHead meals. Or you might want to go **flexitarian**—someone who mostly eats vegetarian, but eats meat sometimes (deciding how often "sometimes" is, that's up to you). Check out Chapter 3, Paths to Veg, for more on the routes you can take to explore your veg curiosity.

If you scored 16–25, being a **Red Head** may suit you best. While there's no official name for it, giving up red meat but still eating chicken and other white meat along with fish is a pretty common choice (especially for those concerned about lowering cholesterol and improving heart health). Some people think of it as a form of flexitarianism, but if you're making the specific decision to just not eat red meat, I say give it its own name. If you're a Red Head, you like vegetables and are willing to eat more of them…but you're not sure you can exist on plants alone. Fair enough! Say so long to steak, buh-bye to burgers, and ta-ta to tartare (if raw meat was your thing to begin with, that is), and see how it feels.

If you scored 26–34, you may want to try out being a **Pescetarian** (pes-ka-tarian). Generally, pescetarians give up meat of all types except for fish. You and meat are mostly through—but tuna subs and California rolls can be such convenient meals! What's more, fish has some great health benefits (including promoting healthy skin, hair, and good mood) that you may not want to miss out on. So, since you're open to change but have an appetite for some things that are familiar, take pescetarianism out for a spin—it just may be your happy place.

If you scored 35–39, being a **Lacto-Ovo Vegetarian** might be right for you (for the record, this is the official name). Lacto-ovos don't eat meat or fish at all, but they do eat animal products such as dairy and eggs. You're all about letting cows and chickens live—but the thought of drinking their milk or eating their eggs doesn't rattle you. You do want to have a significant environmental impact, though, which going meat-free will accomplish. And since you have a curious personality and are flexible when it comes to food, you're well suited to live deliciously, meat-free.

If you scored 40+, you may be ready to take the leap to being **Vegan**: abstaining from eating all animal products including meat, fish, dairy, eggs, and honey; depending on your commitment, it may also extend to avoiding products that come from animals such as beeswax candles and silk scarves. Since you make green living and animal activism top priorities, going vegan may be right for you. You are also adventurous and love trying new foods, which will be crucial to how you'll look and feel, considering the strict dietary restrictions that come along with skipping out on all animal foods. And as for those limitations—they don't stress you out one bit. You're independent and can rely on yourself to make sure there's always something healthy for you to eat, even if it means carrying around a jar of peanut butter "just in case." You will do whatever it takes so that your actions match your morals, and the way you eat is no excuse.

Regardless of your score, what if you have strong feelings that animals should be raised in a way that is respectful of and healthy for them and the people that eat them, is not harmful to the environment, is humane for workers, and provides a fair wage to the farmer—but you believe that it's OK for people to eat meat, dairy, and eggs? You may be an **Conscious Carnivore**. If you want to limit the animal foods you eat to products that have been raised according to the standards listed above (often referred to as sustainable practices), this is the term we'll use to describe you. And if this is you, consider yourself lucky. As recently as ten years ago, you may have been left with no option other than to give up animal foods altogether. Today, however, things have changed—many food producers, grocery stores, and even some restaurants are making it easier for you to eat meat in a way that someone who cares deeply about animals and the environment can feel good about. And for readers who think it's totally backward to say someone takes animal welfare seriously yet eats meat, I say back off. Vegging out isn't for everyone—but everyone benefits from a world where food is produced ethically and sustainably.

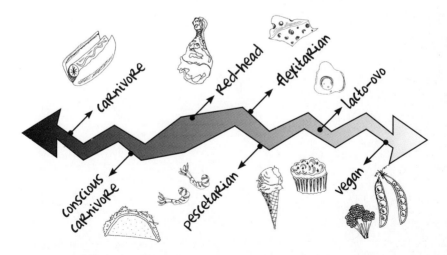

· CHAPTER 2 ·

MYTHS AND REALITIES ABOUT GOING VEGETARIAN

JUST THE FACTS—YOU TAKE
IT FROM THERE.

There are more misconceptions about going veg out there than Lady Gaga has wardrobe changes. Before you head down your chosen path of meatlessness, you deserve to know the true impact of your decision—no agenda, no bias. I give you the facts, and you take it from there.

"BECOMING A VEGETARIAN IS A SUREFIRE WAY TO GET SKINNY."

MYTH

It sounds logical enough—if you give up one entire food category, extra pounds will just fall off your body, right? Nope, not true (as amusing as it is to imagine what that would look like). Losing or gaining weight is a balancing act: calories in vs. calories out. Eating more calories than you burn results in extra poundage; take in fewer calories than you burn and you lose weight. While you may be subtracting meat from your diet, the foods you replace it with will determine your body's energy balance. And even though many vegetarian foods are super low calorie (like carrots and celery), others are not (Snickers bars and cheese fries).

There's another layer to how going veg can impact your weight: the protein piece of the puzzle. Protein—the nutrient that meat, fish, eggs, and cheese are so rich in—is one of the most important factors in satiety (say-tie-ity). Say what? Satiety is the state of being satisfied, or how you should feel at the end of a meal and for a few hours afterward. The less satiated you feel, the more likely you are to hit the vending machine between meals or overdo it the next time you eat. Often when people go veg, they forget about satiating protein. And while pasta with tomato sauce may seem like a healthy lunch choice, unless you add in some protein—like chickpeas, soy meatballs, or a Greek yogurt for dessert—you may find yourself scrounging around for *Lunch: The Sequel* before the final bell of the day has rung. The result? You wind up with an oversupply of energy that your body stores in the form of pounds (check out page 15 or 36 for more on the all-important nutrient protein).

"A MEAT-FREE DIET IS BETTER FOR THE ENVIRONMENT."

REALITY

Even if you've never been to a cattle ranch, you can imagine all of the hard work and energy that is expended to raise animals. First somebody has to grow food for them to eat, like grass or corn. If the animals get sick, they need medication to help them get healthy. Eventually, they are brought to the slaughterhouse; the meat is then kept cool and transported to a butcher and eventually to your dinner plate. Scientists have calculated just how much of an environmental impact all of those steps have, a concept they call "fossil fuel calories." When we burn fossil fuels (which is how most of the world gets energy for everything from cars to air-conditioning), we create around 90 percent of the earth's greenhouse gasses that are trapping excess heat in the earth's atmosphere—in other words, we contribute in a major way to climate change. It takes twenty-five calories of fossil fuels to raise each edible calorie of animal protein (meat, eggs, milk). On the other hand, much less work is required to "raise" plant-based protein—it takes just two fossil fuel calories per edible calorie. As a result, the less animal food you eat, the lower your environmental impact—vegans contribute on average 42 percent fewer greenhouse gas emissions than meat-eaters, lacto-ovo vegetarians 28 percent, and pescetarians around 24 percent, semi-vegetarians around 20 percent, according to a study from Loma Linda University.

And now, a detail I've just got to share because it's way too weird and fascinating not to. When cows burp and fart (I'm serious here) they release methane into the atmosphere. Methane is a potent (ha!) greenhouse gas, a compound that traps heat in the earth's atmosphere, which makes such impolite behavior a huge factor in climate change. Until someone invents Beano for Bovines, simply eating less meat may be the surest way to make sure less methane gets released into the atmosphere (if people eat less meat, eventually the number of cattle raised will shrink, along with their stink). Oh, and if you're concerned about your own, ahem, impact, fear not—most people don't release methane in their personal gas (but remind your little brother he should still keep it quiet, sheesh!).

"VEGETARIAN DIETS ARE WAY HEALTHIER THAN OMNIVOROUS ONES."

MYTH

Any diet you choose—from meat-eating to vegan and everything in between—has the potential to be health-boosting or health-busting. A tub of movie theater popcorn doused with buttery topping (they don't call it butter because, well, it's usually not—more likely it's a mixture of hydrogenated oil and artificial butter flavor) and a pack of Swedish Fish is not exactly the picture of perfect health—but it *is* considered completely vegan by most. Regardless of where you fall on the veg spectrum, it is up to you to make choices that add up to a balanced, healthy diet. We'll get to what that really means and how you can make it happen in Chapter 4, Nutrition for Veggies.

"TOFU—ICK. I COULDN'T POSSIBLY BE A VEGETARIAN."

MYTH

OK, take this as a warning. Once you declare yourself a vegetarian, well-meaning friends and relatives will take it upon themselves to point out the one tofu-containing item on the menu whenever you dine out. Every. Time. For the rest of your life. For whatever reason, people associate vegetarian eating with tofu. Does that mean you have to eat it? Absolutely not.

Many people assume VegHeads crave tofu because they are used to seeing meat as the center of a meal—and tofu, with its semisolid texture and chameleon-like flavor, seems like a suitable meat replacement. It's also a good source of protein, the satiating, muscle-building nutrient that meat is also rich in. (All tofu is, for the record, is soy milk that's been processed in pretty much the same way milk is turned into cheese.) Of course, if it doesn't make it to your mouth, which it won't if you can't stand the stuff, your body gets none of these benefits. Lucky for you, there are plenty of other friendly protein sources out there. To name just a few: almonds, baked beans, black beans, cashew nuts, cheese, chick peas, edamame, eggs, yogurt, hummus, kidney beans, lentils, peanut butter, quinoa, seitan, soy milk, sunflower seeds, tempeh, veggie burgers, veggie chili, veggie hot dogs, walnuts.

Of course (hear me out!), it's possible that if you don't like tofu, it's because you haven't had it prepared well. On its own, the white stuff is about as bland as a food can possibly be. The nice thing about tofu is that it takes on the flavor of the foods it's cooked with, which means that, done right, it might even be considered tasty. If you're looking to give it another try, check out Chapter 10 for recipes like Protein-Packed Parmigiana and Chocolate Power Mousse that may cause you to reconsider your antitofu stance (don't worry, it's still OK to roll your eyes when your mom points out the Tofu Surprise at the local diner for the eighteenth time).

"GOING VEGAN WILL HELP CLEAR UP MY SKIN."

MAYBE

This is a tough one. It turns out that even dermatologists who study this sort of thing can't seem to agree on the role going veg can play in preventing acne.

I decided to sift through some scientific journals to get to the bottom of this for all of my readers—you know, just a bit of light summer reading. According to several studies, there is a link between diet and acne. Scientists theorize that hormones found in dairy foods like milk and cheese can cause your body to overproduce the chemicals that cause breakouts. Even dairy that is raised without the use of growth hormones still contains hormones that are found naturally in milk. Meat also contains hormones. So how much is too much? Well, it's hard to say—everyone is different, say researchers.

Another food factor that can impact your skin is sugar and refined carbohydrates (think white bread and pasta). Eating a high-sugar, high-refined-carb diet jacks up your blood sugar levels, which promotes the production of hormones called androgens that lead to acne.

So it's possible that cutting the meat and dairy in your diet, either completely or just a bit, can help improve your skin. However, eating a lot of carb- or sugar-heavy foods in their place may cancel out any positive changes you might have seen. And of course, other foods (for example, chocolate) you eat might contribute in other ways. Bottom line: it's complicated. There are no guarantees when it comes to any diet and your skin—but no matter what type of diet you follow (veggie or not), be sure to keep sugar as a treat and not a major food group.

"AREN'T VEGETARIANS ALL TREE-HUGGING HIPPIES?"

MYTH

People choose to go veg for all sorts of different reasons—but conforming to one specific "type" is not one of them. Just a sampling of some of the famous (crunchy granola-free) celebs who are reported to be—or have been at one point—proud VegHeads: Carrie Underwood, Natalie Portman, Russell Brand, Kristen Wiig, Ellen DeGeneres, Olivia Wilde, football player Tony Gonzalez, Lea Michele, Milo Ventimiglia, Kristen Bell, Jessica Chastain, Aimee Teegarden, Simon Cowell, baseball player Prince Fielder, WWE Superstar Daniel Bryan, Leona Lewis, Alicia Silverstone, Rooney Mara, Lauren Bush Lauren, ultra-runner Scott Jurek, Kal Penn, Tobey Maguire, Anne Hathaway, mixed martial arts fighter Mac Danzig, Joss Stone, Chelsea Clinton, Jack Johnson, Emily Deschanel, Rachel Meltzer Warren, MS, RDN (OK, OK, I'm not famous—just making sure you're still reading!).

"VEGETARIANS CAN'T POSSIBLY GET ENOUGH PROTEIN."

MYTH

People in the United States have a serious protein problem. That is, they overestimate just how much protein we really require. Yes, the nutrient is important. But in reality, a healthy teen only needs 0.85 grams of protein per kilogram of body weight (each pound equals roughly 0.45 kg). Between the ages of four and thirteen, you need slightly more—around .95 grams per kilogram. So to figure out your protein needs, take your weight in pounds, divide it by 2.2 to get kilograms, and then multiply that number by 0.85 or 0.95. So if you weigh 100 pounds: 100/2.2 = 45.5 x 0.85= 38.7 grams of protein per day. Very informative, you're thinking— but what does that mean foodwise? Well, one plain ol' hamburger at Five Guys Burgers and Fries provides 39 grams—slightly more than a hundred-pounders' daily need (and that's not including the protein in a slice of cheese if you make that order a cheeseburger). For people who eat meat regularly, it's easy to get far more protein than you need on your plate.

So what about if your meals are meat-free? Well, there are plenty of protein options for you too. While few of them contain quite as much protein per serving as meat does, if you eat a well-balanced diet you will likely get just the right amount of protein over the course of the day (around forty-six grams for most teen girls). Here is a list of both animal- and plant-based protein-containing foods, so you can see how easy it is to go veg and still keep up (and how easy it is for meat, meat, and more meat-eaters to go overboard).

FOOD/SERVING SIZE	GRAMS OF PROTEIN
Chicken breast/3.5 oz	30 g
Salmon/3.5 oz	25 g
Egg/One large	6 g
Yogurt, Greek/6 oz	17 g
Milk, lowfat/1 c	9 g
Cheddar cheese/¼ cup shredded	7 g
Tofu, firm/4 oz	8 g
Peanut butter/2 tbsp	8 g
Walnuts/1 oz	4 g
Lentils/½ c	9 g
Chickpeas/½ c	7 g
Quinoa, cooked/1 c	8 g
Broccoli, cooked/1 c	4 g

Short disclaimer: If you are a very, very bad VegHead and eat nothing but pasta and garlic bread, you will NOT be getting enough protein. You don't have to sweat it out to get the right amount of protein, but you can't be a dope about it, either. BALANCE is the key word here. Check out Chapter 4, Nutrition for Veggies, for more on getting all the nutrients you need.

How Much Protein Do I Need?

To calculate your protein needs:
[Your weight in pounds] divided by 2.2 = [your weight in kilograms]
[Your weight in kilograms] x [0.95 if you're 13 or younger] OR [0.85 if you're 14-18] OR [0.8 if you're 19+] = grams of protein you need per day

"IT'S HYPOCRITICAL TO BE A VEGETARIAN AND WEAR LEATHER."

MYTH

OK, in MY opinion this is a myth. Here's why: what you choose to eat and what you choose to wear are both YOUR business. Maybe you don't like the taste of meat, but cows have just never given you the warm and fuzzies. Perhaps there's a health or religious reason you go meatless that doesn't impact what type of shoes you wear. People go veg for many reasons and on many different levels—and no one has the right to tell you that their observance is better than yours.

Beyond that, just because you choose to eat one way today, there's no telling what you'll do tomorrow. So should you abandon plans to go veg if you're not ready to take the plunge completely? Is it wrong to eat vegan and still wear the same old leather gym shoes? I. Think. Not. Dip your toe in whichever end of the veggie pool that speaks to you and see where it goes. And don't worry about what anyone else has to say about it. I've got your back, completely.

That said, many feel that by definition a vegan is a person who not only passes on meat, eggs, dairy, and honey, but also opts not to wear leather, wool, or silk, as those fabrics are made from animals. So if you say you are vegan, people may be surprised to see you keeping warm in a wool scarf. If you eat only vegan foods but choose to wear clothing that comes from animals, it may make your life easier if you are more specific with your explanation for why you're saying "no franks" to the mini hot dogs at your friend's sweet sixteen: "I eat a vegan diet" or "I don't consume anything that came from an animal" rather than "I am a vegan" will explain your choices just fine.

· CHAPTER 3 ·

PATHS TO VEG

BEGIN AT <u>YOUR</u> BEGINNING,
AND IT WILL ALL MAKE
SENSE FOR YOU.

The question on the minds of many veg-curious teens is "but where do I begin?" When I interviewed teens from across the veg spectrum about how to minimize the meat you eat, I got the same answer from them each time: start at the place that feels right to you.

Some of the teens I spoke with started slow to get a taste for their new way of eating. Others have felt more comfortable diving right in to the deep end. There are many different routes you can take. It's also important to keep in mind that the tool you use to transition into your happy veg place can evolve over time as you find your way and settle on the diet that works best for you. None of these approaches is etched in stone. Begin at *your* beginning, and it will all make sense for you.

Below are six different approaches for going from a red-blooded, meat-eating American teen to a red-blooded, meat-avoiding one. (And while we're on the topic—why do people say that anyway? Isn't blood red regardless of what you eat? Anyway...)

MEATLESS MONDAYS

BEST APPROACH IF:

☀ You want to try going veg with little commitment.

☀ The adults in your life don't support your plans to go veg, and you want to show them how easy and healthy it can be.

☀ You want to eat less meat but don't necessarily want to give it up altogether.

Just like "Just Do It" promotes Nike and "I'm Lovin' It" makes you think McDonald's, Meatless Monday is an advertising campaign. While it's been getting a lot of attention in the last few years, it's actually been around since World War I, when it was used by the government to encourage people to eat less meat to save money for the country and conserve resources for soldiers. In 2003, a health advocate got the idea to revitalize Meatless Monday as a campaign to promote public health. With the support of the Johns Hopkins Bloomberg School of Public Health, Meatless Monday has gotten a lot of attention worldwide as a low-commitment, minimal-drama way to reduce the amount of meat in our diets.

Even if you haven't heard of it already, you probably can guess how Meatless Monday works based on its name. The idea behind the campaign is easy—start each new week off with one meat-free day. Not only do you get to test going veg, you also get to show your parents, coach, and others who may think "but it's so hard to be a vegetarian!" that it's really not difficult at all. And according to the people who run Meatless Monday, giving up meat even just once a week can have many of the same benefits to your health and the environment as giving up meat altogether can—so you get to exercise some of those "go green" muscles you've been wanting to put into use.

Get started: Pick a Monday to start going meatless. The weekend before, take a little time to prepare. Explain your plans to your family and see if they'd like to get on board with you. Come to the conversation armed with ideas for how to make this easy on everyone. If your dad always makes you a turkey sandwich for your brown bag lunch, ask for PB + J instead. And offer to make your family's dinner—few parents will pass up the opportunity to put their feet up and relax while you get a meal on the table! If you or your parents are stumped as to what to make for a meal, check out Chapter 10, Get Cookin', VegHead Style, for plenty of delicious options even meat-maniacs will love, or Google "Meatless Monday recipes" for loads of blogs, websites, and Pinterest boards packed with tasty ideas.

THE RED HEAD

BEST APPROACH IF:

- You are ready to make a full-time commitment, but want the flexibility of eating some meat.
- You really like chicken and turkey and only want to give up beef and/or pork.
- You eventually want to go "all the way" veg or vegan, but prefer to make changes gradually.

When it comes to going veg, there are many who get started by giving up red meat first—or who stop eating beef and pork and find that's where their VegHead wants to rest (there's no official name for it, but we'll just call it "Red Head" here). Sharon, twenty-one, of Newark, DE, first stopped eating pork when she was fifteen. When she went to college, she found that the burgers, meat sauce, and other beef foods in the dining hall tasted "pretty bad," and so she stopped eating all red meat. For plenty of people, avoiding red meat is plenty of commitment. Sharon, however, took it a step further. Later that year, she ordered her favorite chicken sandwich at Panera Bread. "I realized I'd scraped all the meat off and was just eating the bread!" she remembers. For Sharon, going Red Head was the first stop on her journey to full-fledged vegetarianism.

Giving up red meat appeals to many because it's a heck of a lot easier than giving up meat altogether. While it may sometimes be hard to find a vegetarian option on a menu or on the buffet table at a party, you can almost always find something that has chicken, turkey, or fish in it. Rejecting red meat can also be a pretty healthy move, since red meat tends to be high in bad-for-your-heart saturated fat—but since you're still eating meat, you're likely getting plenty of protein and nutrients that some vegetarians may have trouble getting enough of.

Being a Red Head is a perfect place for many VegHeads to land indefinitely. And if it's just a layover on your veggie voyage like it was for Sharon, it serves a crucial role. Limiting your diet one step at a time can help you prove to the adults in your life—and yourself—that you can handle the bigger commitment of going fully veg or vegan, if that's where your little veggie-filled heart takes you. Whether or not Red Head is your ultimate goal, you should feel empowered and proud of your decision to take charge of the way in which you're choosing to eat.

Get started: You may have been in the Brownies, but the Boy Scout motto comes in handy for this path: be prepared. Tell your parents that this is something you'd like to do, and explain your reasons. And while you may have known you were headed in this direction, the people around you may not—so ready yourself for any response. "At first my parents thought I was joking," says Jemma, fourteen, of Merrick, NY. "I had to start refusing to eat meals for them to understand I meant business." Begin having conversations about this move with them—the more you talk about it (out loud!), the more seriously they will take you. And just so Mom doesn't think your admirable decision is going to turn her into a short-order cook, be sure to explain what you plan to do when the rest of the family is eating hamburgers (to help you figure out what you can do, check out Chapter 5 for more on meatless meal building).

THE FLEXITARIAN

BEST APPROACH IF:

- ☀ You're not sure where you want to be, but you know that eating less meat is part of your goal.
- ☀ You don't want to be tied down by specific limitations about days of the week or types of food you eat.
- ☀ You're a "go with the flow" person who wants to figure things out as you move forward rather than have them all figured out from the start.

Also known as "semi-vegetarian," flexitarian is a relatively new word that refers to a vegetarian who eats meat occasionally. How often is occasionally? Well, there's no official limit. So if you're committed to the idea of eating less meat but haven't really figured out what that means to you, set out on your road to veg as a flexitarian. "I consider myself a flexitarian because I know it's healthier and better for the environment to eat less meat," says June, fifteen, of St. Louis, MO. "But I don't feel ready to never eat meat at all. I probably eat it about once or twice a week, when I'm at home with my family. When I'm at school or with my friends and I'm in control, I hardly ever eat any."

Get started: Take eating a plant-based diet out for a test drive. Try ordering veg-friendly meals when you eat out or when you get lunch at school to cut down on your meat consumption. And at home, suggest meals that just happen to be vegetarian for everyone to enjoy together—check out Chapter 10 for some delicious ideas everyone will love.

THE VEGXCEPTION

BEST APPROACH IF:

❋ You want to do it...but there's one or two meat-containing foods that you just can't imagine giving up.

Many of the VegHeads I interviewed had one or two foods that were keeping them from going veg or had kept them from it in the past. But if there is one rule for going veg that I want you to take from this book, it's that there really are no rules. You are responsible for figuring out what works for you. As eighteen-year-old Andy from Oakland, CA, put it, "don't feel bad about occasionally eating meat. Do what will make you happy. It's not a rule, it's a lifestyle."

So, will people look at you funny if you say you're a vegetarian and then eat a bowl of Mom's chicken soup at every holiday dinner (as some grown-up VegHeads in my family do)? Well, they might. But that doesn't mean you should throw in the towel and eat meat year-round. If anyone gives you a hard time, smile proudly and tell them: "This is my one vegxception. I don't eat any other meat products." They'll understand.

And keep in mind—the way in which you eat is something that is always evolving. Giving up meat with one vegxception may help you transition to an eventual meat-free diet, if that's your goal. Sarah, eighteen, from Carmel, NY, gave up meat when she was nine with two vegxceptions—her grandmother's meatballs and ham. (Grandma is either an amazing cook or very, very persuasive. Maybe both.) "That was only a couple of times a year, and after about one year of cutting everything out except those two things, I realized I was being silly. So I cut everything out completely. I don't miss it at all!"

Get started: Be up front about your plans. Sure, what you eat is your business. But if you intend to include mini hot dogs on special occasions, why not save yourself the explanations down the road? The benefit is that people will realize you're not making it up as you go along and may take your preferences more seriously instead of nudging you to follow that hot dog with a hamburger, since they can see that "you're eating meat now."

THE COLD TOFURKY

BEST APPROACH IF:

- ⚝ It hit you like a ton of bricks that you just don't want to eat meat any more.
- ⚝ You are in control of most of what you eat; perhaps you live on your own, or you do a lot of the cooking at home.
- ⚝ You're ready!

Quite a few VegHeads I interviewed had an "aha" moment that made them never, ever want to eat meat again. For some, it was watching a movie like *Food, Inc.* or *Forks Over Knives*. Samantha, fifteen, from Philadelphia, PA, went out for dim sum with her family and was grossed out by people eating duck that still, well, looked pretty much like a duck. For Natalie, fourteen, from Merrick, NY, it was a quote from *The Fault in Our Stars* by John Green, about a romance between two teenagers who meet in a kids-with-cancer support group. "It said, 'I want to minimize the number of deaths I am responsible for.' That quote hit me, and the very night I heard that, I stopped eating meat," says Natalie.

Other veg-curious teens jumped into their eating style of choice after some serious consideration—this might make sense for you if you have a life change that makes a once off-limits veg diet suddenly possible. Emma, twenty, from Dallas, TX, wanted to go vegan but her parents disagreed. When she went to college, she saw that the food choices were plentiful—her dining hall offered soy milk for cereal and always had at least one completely plant-based option for meals. On her third day of college, she became vegan and says she has not regretted her decision once (though it can be a challenge when she goes home for school breaks).

Get started: While this approach doesn't require a lot of preparation, it's helpful to have given such a major shift some thought beforehand. You've already made a smart decision by picking up this book to help you navigate the nutritional, social, and other challenges that come with going veg. If you're in the "I just can't do it anymore" camp and don't want to think too much, well, then go for it—and read fast!

THE CONSCIOUS CARNIVORE

BEST APPROACH IF:

☀ Eating meat doesn't bother you, but you want the animals you consume to have lived happy, healthy lives.

☀ You don't want to give up meat, but you want to eat in a way that is good for the environment.

Maybe you're turned off by the practices used to farm meat in this country. You feel that it's OK for us to eat animals, but that they should be treated with some respect and raised in a way that minimizes harm to the environment. Just a few years ago, this may have been enough of a reason to go veg—it was hard to find meat that was up to your standards, and so eating none was your best bet. Not so much anymore. "We are so lucky to live in a time with so many food options!" says Veronica, twenty, of Emeryville, CA. She doesn't consider herself a vegetarian (in fact, she says she eats meat pretty often)—but as far as this book is concerned, she's on the VegHead spectrum with the rest of us. The reason? Veronica has really thought about what role meat should play in her life. And all of that thinking has led her to make some important decisions.

Veronica doesn't like the way that large food corporations push smaller food companies and farms out of business and the negative impact they have on the environment. She's seen photographs of feedlots and slaughterhouses and thinks animals deserve better treatment. As a result, Veronica only eats meat out if it's "humane" or "environmentally conscious." At home, her family shops at farmers' markets, buying meat that was raised locally on organic farms.

Get started: Read the following section, "Conscious Carnivores," for the basics on what it means to be a meat eater with a veg head and for details on how you too can set forth on that path.

Conscious Carnivores: The New Breed of VegHead

Teenagers today think about food a lot more than teenagers in any previous generation. The reason: food is a much bigger part of the public's consciousness than it ever has been. Flip through the TV channels and there are numerous culinary shows to choose from. You can probably name five celebrity chefs without thinking too hard. You've likely seen a movie like *Super Size Me* or *Food Inc.*, or read a book like *Fast Food Nation* or *The Omnivore's Dilemma*. Not to mention all of the food-related blogs, Pinterest boards, and websites that leave you salivating. Given all of this foodtastic information you've, ahem, digested, it may have struck you that the food industry has some dirty little secrets.*

*If you don't know much about how food is produced and want to learn more, there's a ton of information out there. The books and movies mentioned above are good places to start. For more information on them and others, check out Chapter 9, Really Cool Resources.

So what does it mean to be an conscious carnivore? Well, that's for each ethical eater to determine for his or herself. There are a number of different criteria that people who follow an ethical meat-eating diet tend to look for (keep in mind that the definition of each of these standards is subject to change, but the definitions listed in this section were accurate as this book went to press). You can stick with the ones that seem the most relevant to you, or just do your best to eat as ethically as you can, as much as possible. Below, some of the terms worth looking out for (just some of the labels out there):

Organic/Certified Organic: The United States Department of Agriculture (USDA) oversees this label, which means that food producers who use it are held to a high standard. Animals raised organically must eat 100 percent organic feed and have access to the outdoors. The USDA also limits organic food producers from using synthetic pesticides, antibiotics, and genetically modified organisms.

Natural: This term is not as meaningful. It generally indicates that meat doesn't contain artificial flavoring or coloring and minimally processed. However, the word "natural" tells you nothing about the conditions in which an animal was raised. And the government doesn't oversee the use of the term in the same way it supervises use of the word "organic"—so there are no guarantees when you see it used.

Free-Range (or free roaming): This term is regulated by the USDA regarding chickens raised for meat; however there is no legal definition when it applies to egg-laying hens. It means that the animals have had access to the outdoors—though the type of outdoor space and length of time they spend in the sun are not specified.

Cage-Free: This nonregulated term typically means that hens live in an open area (like a barn or warehouse) with unlimited access to food and water. They have more room to spread out than if they were in cages, but they don't necessarily have access to the outdoors.

Pasture-raised: The government does not oversee the use of this term; however, it is usually used to mean that animals have access to the outdoors and get their nutrition the way they do in nature—from grass, plants, and even insects. The meat and eggs from legitimately pasture-raised animals are more nutritious for us. Raising animals in this manner—if companies do as they promise—is also healthier for the animals and better for the environment.

Grass-fed: This term refers only to cattle, sheep, goats, and bison. Grass-fed means that the animals get 100 percent of their nutrition from freshly grazed pasture or hay and grass silage rather than grains, which is the primary food for most cattle in this country. It doesn't tell you anything about the conditions under which the animal was raised. Meat that's been raised on grass can be more nutritious than that raised on grain; this practice is also better for the cows and the environment. Look for meat that has been verified grass-fed by the USDA or the American Grassfed Association.

No Hormones Administered: This implies that the people who raised the animals didn't give them any extra hormones over the course of their lives (hormones do occur naturally, so it isn't technically true to say "hormone free," even though plenty of companies do so). Synthetic hormones are usually used to help animals grow bigger or faster. The USDA can verify if a company using this term is telling the truth, though they don't always do so. It's also worth mentioning that the USDA already doesn't allow added hormones to be used in the raising of hogs or poultry. So if you see pork or chicken products that say "no hormones administered," the company is trying to pull a fast one on you (and possibly charge you more for it). The USDA does however permit additional hormones to be used on cows. So a beef product labeled "no hormones administered" may be worth the extra cash.

No Antibiotics Added: This usually means that the people who raised the animals didn't give them any antibiotics over their lifetime. Antibiotics in food are bad for human health, because when we get overexposed to the drugs, the bacteria in our bodies becomes resistant to them—and that means that one day, the prescription your doctor gives you to heal strep throat or a sinus infection may not work.

Certified Humane: This label is certified by the organization Humane Farm Animal Care and is considered very reputable. To be certified under this program, animals must be raised without growth hormones and antibiotics. They must also have access to clean and sufficient food and water and a healthy living environment. Producers are also required to comply with specific earth-friendly criteria and humane slaughtering standards.

Certified Naturally Grown: Not to be confused with the mostly meaningless "natural," this label is an alternative to the USDA's organic certification. You might see it on produce, honey, poultry, and eggs. The regulations are similar to those for organics, but this program is tailored to meet the needs of smaller-scale farms. Use of the Certified Naturally Grown label is overseen by the organization that administers it, and people consider it to be pretty reputable.

Animal Welfare Approved: This label is designed to ensure that animals live as naturally as possible—in order for products to be certified, the animals raised must been raised outdoors using sustainable farming methods, and meet a stringent list of standards designed by scientists, veterinarians, and farmers. Supervised by the nonprofit Animal Welfare Institute, this label is considered to be reputable.

Five ways to eat more ethically (for carnivores and vegivores)

<u>Find a Farmers' Market</u>: The food that is sold at your local farmers' market is grown close to home, which means that less gas, oil, and other resources are being used to get dinner on your plate. And chances are your friendly neighborhood farmer is using more sustainable practices than the large-scale ranch that ships truckloads of ground beef to your local Walmart. You'll also be helping to keep area farmers in business.

<u>Join a CSA</u>: It stands for Community Supported Agriculture, and you can think of it as a membership in the "vegetables of the week club." Here's how it works: you purchase a share from a farmer for a season. Each week you get a box of whatever produce is harvested that week (there are CSAs for foods like meat, eggs, and dairy, but most are for fruits and veggies). By being a member of a CSA, you get many of the same benefits of shopping at a farmers' market with the added bonus of supporting one farmer's work for an entire season (it also doesn't hurt that it will help your family save money on groceries in the long run, since buying this way tends to be inexpensive and cuts down severely on your grocery needs). Oh, and the biggest bonus: being in a CSA guarantees you a steady supply of super fresh, seasonal food. Delicious.

<u>Look for Local</u>: You're already accomplishing this if you're shopping at a farmers' market or have joined a CSA. But it doesn't have to stop there. You can support local farmers and businesses at the regular grocery store too. Even large chains are starting to disclose where food comes from. Vote

with your dollar and spend your money on food that was grown or produced nearby, whether that's in your county, state, or within a one-hundred-mile radius. You'll be minimizing the environmental impact of your diet with every bite.

Inquire and Applaud: As you learned from the terms covered in this chapter, sometimes foods that are labeled in a way to sound super ethical may not be. And on the other hand, products that don't promote themselves as healthy or ecologically sound may in fact be just so. There's only one way to know what's what, and that's to be an advocate for the things you believe in. Don't be afraid to ask questions—and if you don't get the answers you need, ask some more. If a restaurant says its food is "all natural," ask the owner what that means. If a product at the grocery store sounds suspicious to you, email the company. And if you like what you see—a restaurant serving all Animal Welfare Approved meat, dairy, and eggs, for instance—tell the staff how happy you are to have found them. And then spread the word on your blog, Facebook, web review sites, and Twitter (or write about it in your book...see page 146, Sustainable Spotlight: Grazin').

Grow Your Own: Whether it's in your backyard garden, an urban farm plot, an edible schoolyard, or a pot on the windowsill, you won't find more local veggies than ones you've tended to and harvested yourself.

CHAPTER 4

NUTRITION FOR VEGGIES

ALL IT TAKES IS A LITTLE NUTRITION
KNOW-HOW TO ENSURE THAT YOU'RE
GETTING EVERYTHING YOU NEED.

If I told you that there is one move you can make in life to help you have shiny hair, great skin, a strong, powerful body, an improved mood, and stellar grades, you'd wonder when this morphed from a practical guidebook to a work of fiction. Well, I'm going to go out on a limb and tell you that there *is* a simple way to achieve all those qualities, and you don't even have to take the train to Hogwarts to obtain the magical elixir. The secret, my friends, lies in the foods you eat every day.

Of course, once you set forth on your chosen path to meat-lessness, the idea of selecting the right foods takes on a double meaning: you are faced with the dual tasks of finding foods that fit into your moral, ethical, and taste preferences, as well as ones that will build a diet that will help you thrive. Since the menu of foods you have to pull from is shortened, get-ting the right nutrition can be a bit more of a challenge than it is for someone who eats "everything" (in quotes because no one truly eats everything—the next time someone boasts that they do, ask them if they prefer bull testicle medium-rare or well done). And this minor hurdle has been known to put a veg-hopeful—or more likely, her parents, grandparents, or other adults—unnecessarily on edge.

Let's just clarify one thing right here: being a vegetarian does not mean you're destined to miss out on major nutrients. It also doesn't, as some others believe, put you on the fast track to a healthy diet. Just like someone who eats meat, girls who go veg have to make solid food choices to achieve a balanced diet. Naturally, when you take meat (or more) out of your diet, there are a handful of vitamins and minerals that you become at risk for not getting enough of. But all it takes is a little nutrition know-how to ensure that you're getting everything you need. Let's take a look at the major nutrients of note in a meat-minimal diet: what they are, why they're important, and what to eat to get them.

PROTEIN

When I interviewed veg teens for this book, I asked them what concerned their parents—and themselves—most about their meat-minimal ways of eating. The answer that came up again and again: getting enough protein. Now, don't get me wrong. Protein has its place, and it is crucial you get enough. But when it comes to vegetarian diets, protein is like the most popular girl in school. It gets a lot of attention it *probably* doesn't deserve. Getting an adequate amount of protein isn't as hard as many people think, even when your diet is meat-free—and as I already mentioned, it's certainly not the only nutrient worth your consideration as a VegHead (just like Miss Popularity isn't *actually* the coolest in your class). But since protein is the most likely nutrient to come up in conversation, I'll tackle it first.

Protein is different from the majority of other nutrients highlighted in this chapter because it's a macronutrient, which means that it provides the body with energy (aka calories—the other calorie-containing nutrients are carbohydrates and fat). Most of the other nutrients we'll talk about are micronutrients—vitamins and minerals that your body needs in far smaller amounts. They don't give you energy, but play various crucial roles that help your body to function.

Protein is made up of building blocks called amino acids. While your body can produce some amino acids, it can't make all of them. Those amino acids are considered "essential" for that very reason—it is essential that you eat them. Animal foods like meat and dairy contain all of the essential amino acids while plant-based forms of protein only contain a few of these amino acids at a time. As a result, people used to think that VegHeads had to be careful to combine certain amino acid–containing foods together so their bodies would get all of the essential ones at one meal. Now, we know better—if you eat a variety of foods that contain all of the essential amino acids over the course of the day, you're all set (your body takes care of the combining part—clever, clever body!).

Why It's Important

If you don't get enough or the right balance of protein, your body may break down protein in the body—including your muscles—to obtain the amino acids it needs.

Protein also has a part in how you feel over the short term. Your body digests protein differently than it does carbohydrates and fat, giving your body an increased sense of satiety or fullness. So many VegHeads fall into what I call "the protein trap"—we adjust meat-containing meals to be veg-friendly, and in the process eliminate nearly all the protein from the dish (think spaghetti and meatballs without the meatballs, aka big carb-loaded bowl of spaghetti, or Thanksgiving dinner without the turkey, aka stuffing, mashed potatoes, and candied yams—I know I've done both!). We fill up on carbohydrates, which stuff our bellies, but then find ourselves hungry for more an hour later. Making sure you fill in that protein piece of the puzzle, in other words, replacing the protein you've subtracted with a veg-friendly source of protein, will give your meal some staying power that it wouldn't have had otherwise.

YOUR NEEDS

Around 46 grams per day. Technically you need about 0.95 grams of protein for every kilogram of body weight until you're thirteen; 0.85 grams of protein per kilogram of body weight if you're fourteen to eighteen, and 0.8 grams of protein per kilogram of body weight if you're nineteen or older. To calculate your weight in kilograms, divide the number of pounds you are by 2.2.

VEGHEAD PROTEIN SOURCES

For everyone—kidney beans, black beans, chickpeas (garbanzo beans), lentils, cannellini beans, pinto beans, baked beans, tofu, tempeh, seitan, textured vegetable protein, almonds, walnuts, pine nuts, cashews, peanuts, peanut butter, soy nuts, soy nut butter, edamame (green soy beans), quinoa.

For lacto-ovo veggies—add eggs, milk, regular yogurt, Greek yogurt, kefir, cheese, cottage cheese, ricotta cheese.

For pescetarians—add fish such as salmon, tuna, flounder, cod, tilapia, and halibut, and seafood such as shrimp, scallops, and crab.

For red heads—add chicken and turkey.

YOUR PLANT-BASED DAY, IN PROTEIN

Breakfast: Two slices of whole wheat toast (8 g) with 2 tablespoons of peanut butter (8 g) and a medium banana (1.3 g) = 17.3 g protein

Lunch: 2 avocado and cucumber sushi rolls (3 g) with 1 cup of steamed edamame (17 g) = 20 g protein

Snack: 6 woven wheat crackers (3 g) with ½ cup baby carrots (0.6 g) and ¼ cup hummus (9.7 g) = 13.3 g protein

Dinner: Amy's black bean enchilada with Spanish rice and beans frozen dinner (9 g) and 1 Edy's lemonade fruit bar (0 g) = 9 g protein

Total protein for the day: 63.6 grams protein

[Iron: 13 mg; Calcium: 306 mg; Zinc: 6 mg; Vitamin B12: 0 mcg; Vitamin D: 0 IU; Choline: 161 mg; Omega-3s: 0 g★]

★Note: I've included nutrition information for each of the eight nutrients covered in this chapter in each "your plant-based day" section. The sample diets are examples of how a person might actually eat in a day; while the foods listed provide plenty of the highlighted nutrient, it may be fall short in others. Remember, it's what you eat over the long term that really matters. Use these examples to help you learn how to build the most nutrient-packed diet and clue you in to when you might need to supplement.

Milking It

Beware: While dairy foods like milk and yogurt are typically a good source of protein, vegan substitutes like almond milk and coconut yogurt are often lacking in the nutrient. Soy-based dairy substitutes have the most protein. Read labels to be sure you know what you're getting!

Powder Puff Girl?

If you've spent any time in a gym or at a smoothie stand lately, you may have seen a muscle-bound dude fueling up on a protein powder–laden shake. And with all the talk around VegHeads getting enough protein, you might be wondering if adding a scoop of powder to your blended drinks, oatmeal, soups or other recipes is a smart way to make sure you're getting enough of the nutrient. After all, they're easily available in pharmacies, health food stores, and on the Internet, and come in a range of sources to suit any VegHead diet—from the vegan (soy, pea, hemp) to the lacto-ovo (whey, casein—both from milk—as well as egg). So is protein powder right for you?

Not so fast, veggie girl. If you've read this section on protein (you have read this section, haven't you?), you know that it's really not terribly hard to get enough protein in your diet, even if you're vegan. The advice I always give my clients is that food comes first. In other words, if you can get an adequate amount of a nutrient from your diet, that's always preferable to getting it from a pill or a powder. The reasons: first off, we don't know everything there is to know about nutrition, and by isolating one nutrient from the others it comes packaged with in nature, you may be losing some of the benefit. Similarly, taking one nutrient in a concentrated form means you're bound to get much more of it than you would in any food source—and when it comes to nutrients, too much of a good thing can be too much. In fact, soy protein, while thought to be super healthy when eaten in foods like soy milk, tofu, and tempeh, may stimulate the growth of breast cancer cells when eaten in the form of concentrated supplements, according to research from Northwestern University.

So for now, it's best to make food your first stop for protein. If you're really, really having trouble getting enough, you can consider adding a small amount of protein powder to your diet—but be sure to research the possible risks of the powder you're considering, and to make sure you're still getting plenty of "real food," limit it to no more than one scoop per day.

IRON

While protein is busy getting all of the attention, iron just may be the most important nutrient for girls going veg to take into consideration. Three-fourths of teenage girls in the U.S. don't eat enough of the mineral, and non–meat eaters are at an even greater risk for deficiency since animal products are some of the best sources of it. It's not that teenage girls are so much worse at eating iron-rich foods than people in other age groups; it's that they tend to require more of it. Needs are higher when your body is still growing; they're also higher for women, who lose iron when they get their periods each month. If you find yourself in both categories at the same time, it's a double whammy for your iron needs. In addition, VegHeads have an extra challenge—while plenty of plant foods contain iron, they generally have less of the nutrient than meat does. As well, the type of iron in plant foods, called non-heme iron, is different from the form in animal foods—and our bodies don't absorb it as well as they do the heme iron in meat.

Why It's Important

Iron is found in the hemoglobin, a component of red blood cells, which helps transport oxygen to the body's organs and tissues. When your body doesn't get enough iron, you can develop iron-deficiency anemia—small red blood cells or an inadequate number of them due to a lack of hemoglobin. As a result, your cells don't get enough oxygen and you may feel tired, grumpy, or have trouble focusing.

YOUR NEEDS

If you're nine to thirteen: 8 milligrams per day

If you're fourteen to eighteen: 15 milligrams per day

If you're nineteen and older: 18 milligrams per day

VEGHEAD IRON SOURCES

Everyone—spinach, swiss chard, collard greens, oatmeal, lentils, kidney beans, chickpeas, edamame, pinto beans, almonds, pistachios, sunflower seeds, enriched cereals, blackstrap molasses, figs, raisins, broccoli, tofu, tempeh.

Lacto-ovo—add eggs.

Pescetarian—add clams, mackerel, mussels, oysters, shrimp, trout.

Red Head—add chicken and turkey.

YOUR PLANT-BASED DAY, IN IRON

Breakfast: One packet of instant fortified oatmeal (11 mg) with small box of raisins (1 mg) and ¼ cup chopped walnuts (3 mg) = 15 mg

Lunch: Chipotle Mexican Grill burrito with fajita veggies, white rice, black beans, tomato salsa, lettuce, and guacamole (6 mg) = 6 mg

Snack: Chocolate Chip Cookie Dough Larabar (2 mg) = 2 mg

Dinner: Stir-fried broccoli and red pepper (1 mg) with ½ cup firm tofu (2 mg) and 1 cup soba noodles (1 mg) = 4 mg

Total: 27 mg

[Protein: 63 g; Zinc: 9 mg; Calcium: 765 mg; Vitamin B12: 0 mcg; Vitamin D: 0 IU; Choline: 129 mg; Omega-3s: 11 g]

Power Pairing

Eating a food that's rich in vitamin C along with a food that contains iron helps your body absorb more of the harder-to-use non-heme iron you'll find in plant foods like spinach and chickpeas by as much as six times, making the absorption as good or even better than heme iron from plant foods! Good sources of vitamin C include orange, lime, lemon (and their juices), red bell pepper, tomatoes and tomato sauce, papaya, strawberries, and pineapple. Try combining them with any iron food you eat (it's easy to do, considering that means delicious combos like slicing sweet strawberries on a spinach salad, loads of lemon juice in hummus, and crunchy red pepper in a tofu stir-fry).

ZINC

This mineral is found in all of the organs, tissues, and fluids in your body—from your bones to your kidneys to your skin. Vegetarians might need more zinc than nonvegetarians because a compound called phytate found in grains, nuts, and beans—foods VegHeads tend to eat more of than other people—ties up zinc, interfering with your body's ability to use it (some researchers say that's not really a problem, though it couldn't hurt to get a good amount of zinc just to be on the safe side). Increased needs or not, most vegetarians get between 10 and 30 percent less zinc than meat eaters—so many of us would benefit from adding some zinc-rich foods to our diets.

Why It's Important

Zinc has many important roles in your body. It helps your cells divide and grow, your wounds heal, and even helps your body turn the carbohydrates you eat in foods like pasta and rice into energy. Zinc also helps your immune system keep you healthy, which is why some people may pop zinc supplements when they feel a cold coming on, and is extremely important for your senses of smell and taste.

YOUR NEEDS

If you're nine to thirteen: 8 milligrams per day.

If you're fourteen to eighteen: 9 milligrams per day.

If you're age nineteen and older: 8 milligrams per day.

VEGHEAD ZINC SOURCES

Everyone—tahini, pumpkin seeds, cashews, tofu, tempeh, white beans, chickpeas, lentils, kidney beans, fortified cereals, *nutritional yeast*.

Lacto-ovo—add yogurt, cheese, milk, eggs.

Pescetarian—add oysters, crab, scallops, shrimp, lobster.

Red Head—add chicken, turkey.

YOUR PLANT-BASED DAY, IN ZINC

Breakfast: 1 cup of Rice Chex (3.75 mg) with 1 cup of lowfat milk (1 mg) and ½ cup blueberries (0.25 mg) = 5 mg

Lunch: Hummus sandwich—2 slices whole wheat bread (1 mg) with 1 tablespoon hummus (0.25 mg), ¼ avocado (0.25 mg), and ¼ cup shredded carrots (0 mg) and ¼ cup whole almonds (1 mg) mixed with ¼ c dried apricot halves (0.5 mg) = 3 mg

Snack: 4 cups popcorn (1 mg) sprinkled with 2 tablespoons nutritional yeast (1.5 mg) = 2.5 mg

Dinner: ¾ cup whole wheat rotini (1.25 mg) with ½ cup white beans (1.50 mg) and 1 chopped tomato sautéed in garlic and oil (0.25 mg) = 3 mg

Total = 13 milligrams

[Protein: 55 g; Iron: 25.66 mg; Calcium: 766 mg; Vitamin B12: 5.05 mcg; Vitamin D: 157 IU; Choline: 75 mg; Omega-3s: .04 g]

What the Heck Is...*Nutritional Yeast?*

Totally weird and totally cool, nutritional yeast looks similar to the yellow powder you'll find in some mac n' cheese mixes. It truly is yeast (as in "the stuff that makes bread rise") that's been heated to a high temperature and deactivated. This process brings out its flavor—surprisingly cheesy, which makes it popular among vegans—and nutritional properties—high in protein and zinc, which also makes it a veg favorite. Nutritional yeast is often also fortified with vitamin B12, another nutrient vegans may not get enough of. Try it sprinkled on popcorn or on top of pasta if cheese isn't your thing, or if you're simply looking for something different.

CALCIUM

Teens and tweens need more of this bone-building mineral than adults, since they're still growing—and many don't get enough. If you're vegan or you stay away from dairy foods for any other reason, you're at an even greater risk of falling short. Once, I was explaining to a four-year-old which foods are good sources of calcium. When I listed off the foods that contain the mineral, he responded, "Oh! That's why it's called *cow*cium!" And he was right in that ridiculously cute sort of way preschoolers can be—many of the foods we think of when it comes to calcium do come from cows! The good news for vegans is, you can find cow—er, calcium in plenty of plant-based foods. You just have to think about it a little more than your moo-juice-drinking friends—no milk mustache required.

Why It's Important

Chances are you've heard that calcium is important for building strong bones. But did you know that you build most of the strength of your bones *for life* before you're eighteen years old? After age eighteen, the rate slows down, and after around age thirty, they stop strengthening altogether. Eek! Getting enough calcium now will help prevent bone fractures now and *osteoporosis* later on. It's also important for blood clotting (that's how you stop bleeding when you have a cut) as well as nerve and muscle function. Note: eating a diet that is rich in fruits and vegetables and low in animal protein seems to help strengthen bones. So if you're a healthy vegan, you're in far better shape than if you're a candy-coated one. But bottom line: You. Still. Need. Calcium.

YOUR NEEDS

About 1,300 milligrams of calcium per day.

VEGHEAD CALCIUM SOURCES

Everyone—fortified nondairy milk, fortified nondairy yogurt, fortified orange juice, blackstrap molasses, collard greens, tofu, fortified cereal, kale, broccoli, soybeans, dried figs, almond butter, tahini, tempeh, black beans, baked beans, almonds, fortified oatmeal and Cream of Wheat.

Lacto-ovo—add milk, yogurt, cheese

Pescetarian—add canned sardines, canned salmon (they often contain teensy bones—you may not notice they're there, but they add calcium).

Red Head—n/a

YOUR PLANT-BASED DAY, IN CALCIUM

Breakfast: 2 Kashi toaster waffles (38 mg) with 1 cup strawberry halves (24 mg) and 1 cup fortified OJ (349 mg) = 411 mg

Lunch: 2 slices whole wheat bread (60 mg) with 2 tablespoons almond butter (212 mg) and 1 tablespoon raspberry jelly (4 mg)= 276 mg

Snack: Fignana smoothie (see page 173 for recipe, 370 mg) = 370 mg

Dinner: MorningStar Farms vegetarian corn dog (7 mg) with ½ cup vegetarian baked beans (86 mg) and 1 cup krazy kale chips (see page 218 for recipe, 182 mg) = 275 mg

Total: 1332 mg

[Protein: 55 g; Iron: 11.6 mg; Zinc: 9.5 mg; Vitamin B12: 1.9 mcg; Vitamin D: 6 IU; Choline: 173.8 mg; Omega-3s: 0.06 g]

What the Heck is...*Osteoporosis?*

This refers to a disease in which the bones become very brittle and prone to breaking. It develops over time, and affects older white and Asian women the most.

Should I Take a Calcium Supplement?

I've said it before and I'll say it again: Food first. You're much better off with calcium you get in foods than the type you get in supplements, for various reasons. However, if you can't get close to the recommended 1,300 milligrams per day, you may want to consider a supplement. Look for one that uses "calcium carbonate" or "calcium citrate," which are more absorbable and safer than others. And if you take more than one calcium pill to meet your needs, take them at different times of day—your body will be able to use more that way.

Alternative Bone-builders

Calcium is not the only factor in building strong bones. Many other nutrients you take in and choices you make impact your bones and help prevent osteoporosis. For example:

- Exercise! Any activity that puts force or pressure on your bones pushes them to build themselves stronger. Running, dancing, tennis, yoga, and lifting weights are all great options.
- Skip cigarettes. Smoking is associated with decreased bone density.
- Drink with caution. If you choose to use alcohol once you get old enough, do so wisely. Drinking can interfere with the balance of calcium as well as hormones and vitamins that you need to build strong bones. People who drink over the long term have an increased risk for spine, hip, and wrist fractures.
- Vitamin D helps your body absorb and use whatever calcium

you eat. See page 52 for more on vitamin D and how to make sure you're getting enough.

- Eat plenty of vitamin K, which plays a role in increasing bone density. You can find it in leafy green vegetables like kale, spinach, collard greens, brussels sprouts, and broccoli.

- Load up on the minerals potassium and magnesium—they also play a role in keeping bones strong. Fruits and vegetables are your best bets for getting enough potassium while nuts are an especially good source of magnesium.

VITAMIN B12

Vitamin B12 is found in fish, shellfish, meat, eggs, and dairy—but no plant foods, other than ones that have been fortified. It can be a challenge for vegans to get enough of this important vitamin. Your body stores years' worth of vitamin B12 in the liver, so it's OK if you don't always get exactly enough. And you don't need very much—only 2.4 micrograms per day. If you're not eating any animal foods, you'll want to be sure to add vitamin B12-fortified ones to your diet (or add in a B12 supplement, if fortified foods aren't your thing). If you are a lacto-ovo or other flavor VegHead, it's still a good idea to make sure you're eating enough B12-containing foods. And vegans and lacto-ovo vegetarians should periodically ask their doctors to screen them for B12 deficiency.

Why It's Important

You need vitamin B12 so that your body can form healthy red blood cells, which are important for delivering oxygen to your organs. The vitamin also helps your nervous system function. Not getting enough can cause a type of anemia that may make you feel foggy and out of it; not treated over time it can lead to depression, memory loss, and irritability.

YOUR NEEDS

If you're nine to thirteen: 1.8 micrograms per day.

If you're fourteen or older: 2.4 micrograms per day.

VEGHEAD VITAMIN B12 SOURCES

Everyone—fortified foods like nondairy milk, nondairy yogurt and cereals; fortified meat replacements like Morningstar Farms Meal Starters Grillers Recipe Crumbles.

Lacto-ovo—add eggs, milk, yogurt, cottage cheese.

Pescetarian—add salmon, sardines, crab, trout, tuna, shrimp.

Red Head—add chicken, turkey.

YOUR PLANT-BASED DAY, IN VITAMIN B12

Breakfast: 1 cup of Cheerios (1.9 mcg) with 1 cup fortified soymilk (3 mcg) and 1 peach (0 mcg) = 4.9 mcg

Lunch: Amy's Bean and Rice Burrito (0 mcg) with a lettuce, tomato, cucumber, and avocado salad sprinkled with sunflower seeds (0 mcg) = 0 mcg

Snack: Banana (0 mcg) with peanut butter (0 mcg) = 0 mcg

Dinner: Spaghetti with tomato sauce (0 mcg) and ½ cup Morningstar Farms Meal Starters Grillers Recipe Crumbles. (3.4 mcg) = 3.4 mcg

Total = 8.3 mcg

[Protein: 60 g; Iron: 24 mg; Calcium: 605 mg; Zinc: 11 mg; Vitamin D: 144.54 IU; Choline: 169.6 mg; Omega-3s: 0.66 g]

VITAMIN D

This is one vitamin that most everyone, VegHead or not, has trouble getting enough of. In the United States, around three quarters of all teens are lacking, according to one government survey. Vitamin D is unusual because you don't just get it through your diet—your skin produces it when it's exposed to the sun. But these days, we spend less time outside, and when we do, we (wisely) cover up so we don't get skin cancer. So that equals less vitamin D. Add in the fact that most food sources of vitamin D come from animals, and you'll see why going veg means it's time for you to get with D program when it comes to this crucial vitamin.

Why It's Important

You've already read why calcium is important for bones. Well vitamin D and calcium work as a team. Without enough vitamin D, all of that calcium you're working hard to eat can't be used by your bones. What's more, vitamin D also helps ensure your immune system fends off bacteria and viruses and keeps your brain working well—research has linked a lack of adequate vitamin D with mental illness in teens.

YOUR NEEDS

The National Institutes for Health say we need around 600 IUs per day, though other experts are now saying we need far more. See "Get Tested" for more information (page 54).

VEGHEAD VITAMIN D SOURCES

Everyone—fortified orange juice, fortified cereal, fortified non-dairy milk, certain mushrooms (see box on next page).

Lacto-ovo—add fortified milk and yogurt, eggs.

Pescetarian—add swordfish, salmon, tuna, sardines.

Red Head—n/a

YOUR PLANT-BASED DAY, IN VITAMIN D

Breakfast: 1 ½ cups Total cereal (150 IUs) and 1 cup fortified soymilk (100 IUs) with 1 cup fortified orange juice (140 IUs) = 390 IUs

Lunch: 1 ½ cups lentil soup (0 IUs) with 4 cups of popcorn (0 IUs) = 0 IUs

Snack: So Delicious Strawberry Greek cultured coconut milk yogurt (180 IUs) = 180 IUs

Dinner: Protein-Packed Parmigiana (see page 209 for recipe, 120 IUs) with ½ cup whole wheat spaghetti and 1 cup of steamed broccoli topped with ¼ cup tomato sauce (0 IUs) = 120 IUs

Total = 690 IUs

Get Tested

As you can see, it's hard for most people to get enough vitamin D no matter how veg their head is. And scientists are still debating how much we actually need. To make sure you're getting enough vitamin D, ask your doctor for a simple blood test. If your levels are too low, it may be a good idea for you to add in a vitamin D supplement. Talk with your doctor or dietitian to determine how much is right for you.

D Fungi (The Fun Guy? Get It?)

Mushrooms can be one of the few natural plant-based sources of vitamin D. Like us, they produce vitamin D when exposed to light. Some companies are intentionally shining a special ultraviolet light (like the rays from the sun) on mushrooms so they bulk up on vitamin D before you find them at the store. Ask whoever does the shopping at your house to look for Monterey Mushrooms (www.montereymushrooms.com) or another brand of vitamin D mushrooms.

CHOLINE

You don't hear a lot of talk about choline, mostly because it's found in a lot of foods and people tend to get enough of it without trying too hard. However, it's mostly found in much higher concentrations in animal foods compared with plant foods (particularly eggs), and is definitely a nutrient VegHeads (especially vegans) should be aware of.

Why It's Important

Choline plays an important role in the function of cell membranes. You also need it to make acetylcholine, a neurotransmitter that sends messages from your body's nerves to its muscles.

YOUR NEEDS

If you're nine to thirteen: 375 milligrams per day.

If you're fourteen to eighteen: 400 milligrams per day.

If you're nineteen or older: 425 milligrams per day.

VEGHEAD CHOLINE SOURCES

Everyone—soymilk, quinoa, tofu, edamame, peanut butter, pinto beans, almonds, pistachios, asparagus, brussels sprouts, broccoli, potatoes, chickpeas, baked beans, barley, lentils.

Lacto-ovo—add eggs, milk, yogurt.

Pescetarian—add scallops, shrimp, sardines, cod.

Red Head—add chicken, turkey.

YOUR PLANT-BASED DAY, IN CHOLINE

Breakfast: Barley breakfast cereal—1 cup pearled barley (21 mg) prepared with water and topped with ¼ cup pistachios (22 mg) and 5 dates, chopped (22 mg); one cup of steamed soymilk (57 mg) = 102 milligrams

Lunch: 2 slices whole wheat bread (14 mg) with 2 tablespoons peanut butter (20 mg) and 1 medium banana (12 mg), an orange (15 mg) = 61 milligrams

Snack: 1 cup edamame (88 mg) = 88 milligrams

Dinner: 1 cup quinoa (42 mg) with 1 cup garbanzo beans (80 mg) and ½ cup each broccoli (31 mg) and cauliflower (24 mg) = 177 milligrams

Total = 428 milligrams

[Protein: 73 g; Iron: 16 mg; Calcium: 739 mg; Zinc: 10.43 mg; Vitamin B12: 2.07 mcg; Vitamin D: 104.49 IU; Omega-3s: 1.8 g]

OMEGA-3 FATTY ACIDS

Unless you're a fish-eater, omega-3 fatty acids likely present a challenge. The reason: there aren't many nonfish foods out there that contain EPA and DHA, the two main omega-3 fatty acids (the exception is sea vegetables, which people eat a lot of in Japan, but not so much in our neck of the woods). As a result, lacto-ovo vegetarians and vegans have about half the amount of EPA and DHA in their blood and tissues as nonvegetarians do. There is another omega-3 fatty acid called ALA, which your body is able to convert to EPA and DHA. It is found in plant foods like chia and flaxseeds and walnuts. Unfortunately, our bodies don't break ALA into EPA and DHA very well. Even so, they may be the only way you will get any omega-3s in your diet, and some is better than none.

Why It's Important

Omega-3 fatty acids help prevent inflammation in the body. As a result, they may lower your risk of diseases like heart disease and arthritis. They're also important for helping your brain work, and some studies have found them to protect against depression.

YOUR NEEDS

The Institutes of Medicine suggest that adults get 1.1 to 1.6 grams of ALA per day, though they haven't set a specific recommendation for teens.

VEGHEAD OMEGA-3 SOURCES

Everyone—walnuts, flaxseed, flaxseed oil, chia seed, hemp seed, hemp milk, canola oil.

Lacto-ovo—add omega-3 enriched eggs.

Pescetarian—add fatty fish (salmon, tuna, sardines, halibut).

Red Head—n/a

YOUR PLANT-BASED DAY, IN OMEGA-3S

Breakfast: 1 cup of oatmeal (0 g) prepared with 1 cup of Living Harvest hemp milk (1.11 g), topped with ½ cup sliced strawberries (0 g) and 1 tablespoon ground flaxseed (1.75 g) = 2.86 g

Lunch: Green salad with 2 tablespoons salad dressing (0 g), ¼ cup hummus (0 g) and 2 tablespoons walnuts (1.2 g) = 1.2 g

Snack: Chia power pudding (see page 223 for recipe, 5.05 g) = 5.05 g

Dinner: Grace's Not-ggets (see page 213 for recipe, .97 g) with super sweet potato "fries" (see page 219 for recipe, .23 g) and krazy kale chips (see page 218 for recipe; 0 g) = 1.2 g

Total = 10.31 g

[Protein: 47.18 g; Iron: 7.93 mg; Calcium: 438 mg; Zinc: 5.15 mg; Vitamin B12: 0 mcg; Vitamin D: 0 IU: Choline: 57 mg]

Supplemental Evidence

Some experts recommend that people who don't eat fish at least twice a week should take an omega-3 supplement. Unless that's you, it may be a good idea to supplement. However, most omega-3 pills are made from fish oil, which poses a problem if you're avoiding fish. So, what to do? The answer: get your omega-3s from the same place the fish do—algae! There are a number of vegan omega-3 supplements on the market that are derived from, well, seaweed (as appetizing as that sounds). Here are a few brands to look for:

- Deva
- NulQue
- NuTru
- NutraVege

Veg Teens and Eating Disorders

I can't sit here being your plant-based cheerleader without bringing up the topic of disordered eating in teen girls, particularly those who decide to go veg.

Before we go any further, let's agree on a basic definition of what an eating disorder is. According to Merriam-Webster, it's "any of several psychological disorders characterized by serious disturbances of eating behavior." Anorexia and bulimia, some of the most well-known eating disorders, are most often seen in females in their teens and twenties. What's more, many young women experience a wide range of disordered eating behaviors that may not warrant an official diagnosis but do get in the way of health and happiness. For this reason, any health professional who works with teenage girls—and any adult who cares about a teen girl—has a good reason to be on alert for warning signs for irregular eating behavior.

For some adults, seeing a teenage girl going veg raises a red flag that she may be showing signs of disordered eating—it's true, after all, that a girl who goes veg makes the decision to limit her diet in a big way. And while it's hard for you and me to understand how this doesn't just instantly make sense to everyone (it's better for the planet! it's healthier! it tastes better!), it's just as hard for people who enjoy meat to understand why you'd want to go through life without ever eating another juicy steak. As a result, you may encounter an adult—a parent, coach, or even doctor or registered dietitian nutritionist—who hears you say "I don't want to eat meat," and takes it to mean "I have a serious problem."

Before we get all "how DARE they?!?!?!?" (I know, it's my knee-jerk reaction too—it really is), let's remember that the parents, coaches, doctors, and registered dietitian nutritionists in your life care about you and are trying to look out for your best interests. So is it justified for them to be so skeptical about your dietary choices? Unfortunately, it may be.

Young women diagnosed with an eating disorder were more likely to be vegetarian compared with those who'd never been diagnosed with an eating disorder, according to research published in the *Journal of the Academy of Nutrition and Dietetics*. Another study of eating disorder patients suggested that about half had become vegetarian several years before the onset of their disease. Some psychologists say that a young woman who is in the process of developing an eating disorder might latch on to vegetarianism as a socially acceptable way of restricting her diet.

You may feel like it's totally unfair that an adult whose main concern is your well-being looks at you with a raised eyebrow when you announce that you've gone veg. But eating disorders in vegetarian teens are an unfortunate reality that should be taken into consideration. It's totally uncool when an adult *assumes* that a teenager who is going veg is actually crying out for help (in my experience, most veggie teens are strong-willed, independent-minded, passionate, and über smart young ladies who decide to go meatless because of their beliefs about animals, the environment, and other serious issues, or they simply don't like the taste of meat). Those using vegetarianism as a cover for disordered eating are, I believe, the minority. But with the realities and seriousness of disordered eating in mind, here are a few questions you should ask yourself to determine whether or not you (or any VegHead friend this may apply to) have chosen to go down this path for the right reasons.

ARE YOU GOING VEG TO LOSE WEIGHT?

The list of good reasons for going veg is near endless—taste preference, health, sustainability, and cost are all reasonable explanations. The one reason that's not: weight control. In the *Journal of the Academy of Nutrition and Dietetics* study, 42 percent of vegetarian eating disorder patients said they went veg to help slim down. The percentage of vegetarians without eating disorders who were motivated by weight? Zero. And for good reason: as you know, going veg does not put you on the fast track to a bikini; healthful eating, portion control, and exercise do.

DO YOU SEE MEAT AS A "BAD" FOOD?

Eating meat may not be your preference. And you may be passionate about preventing cruelty toward animals—that's OK. But there is no such thing as a "good" or "bad" food. Diets are made up of choices, some healthier or more green than others—what's important is the overall picture of how you eat. If you find yourself thinking of your meat-eating days as a dark time in your life, you may be seeing things a little too black and white.

DO YOU FEEL LIKE GOING MEATLESS IS A GOOD WAY TO BE PERFECT?

People are not perfect, and there's no such thing as a "perfect" way of eating. But there's a name for the state of being "fixated on righteous eating," called orthorexia nervosa. While orthorexia is not an officially recognized disorder, many health professionals see it as being detrimental in that food choices become so restrictive that health suffers. For people with orthorexia, eating in a certain way may give one a feeling of superiority or purity. If you find yourself viewing vegetarianism or veganism as a means of achieving some higher level of being, feel guilt when you stray from your dietary choices, wonder how others can possibly eat the foods they eat, and feel in control when you eat "correctly," you may be exhibiting orthorexic behavior.

If you're concerned that your going veg may be going too far—or you want some reassurance that it's not—here are a few steps you can take to stay your healthy, happy self:

TALK IT OUT

A trained psychologist will help you sift through your emotions and decide if going veg is an emotionally healthy decision for you. You may be able to meet with one through your school; if not, a guidance counselor, parent, or doctor can help you find someone to work with (in most cases it is covered by insurance). If you're on your own, visit http://therapists.psychologytoday.com to locate a therapist in your area.

GET NUTRITION SUPPORT

Registered dietitian nutritionists (RDN), sometimes called Registered Dietitians (RD) are the most highly qualified nutrition professionals out there—they've completed a significant amount of approved coursework and an intensive supervised practice program, passed a national registration exam, and keep up to date with ongoing continuing education. Most also have advanced degrees and additional training. When you meet with an RDN, she will discuss your diet to help you make sure you're making the right choices, much like the information provided in Chapter 5 of this book—but since you're in person, she'll be able to give you personalized recommendations tailored to your exact needs, likes, and dislikes. Just don't assume that all RDNs are created equal. I recommend finding one who is supportive of vegetarian diets. Visit www.eatright.org/programs/rdfinder to locate an RDN in your area, then click on "view details" to choose one who lists "vegetarian nutrition" as a specialty.

FIND JOY IN FOOD

Contrary to popular belief, going veg isn't about what you're not eating—it's about what you *are* eating. (That's why it's called vegetarian and not "no meat-atarian." OK, I made that up. But you get the point.) Instead of fixating on the foods you've removed from your diet, focus on the delicious ones you've added. And make a point of finding ways to enjoy these new finds (loads of ideas in Chapter 10, Get Cookin', VegHead-Style, starting on page 167), whether you're the one in the kitchen or you're printing up recipes from the *Vegetarian Times* website for Mom or Dad to try. Embracing the fun in food allows going veg to be a choice that enhances your life rather than something that limits it.

· CHAPTER 5 ·

BUILDING YOUR VEGETARIAN MEAL

IT'S NOT YOUR JOB TO CONVERT
YOUR FAMILY TO YOUR EATING
HABITS, JUST AS IT'S NOT THEIR
PLACE TO GET YOU TO CHANGE.

Now that we've spent all this time reviewing key vitamins and minerals, it's time I let you in on a little secret we registered dietitian nutritionists have—we don't eat nutrients, we eat food. Food is made up of nutrients, of course (well, most of it is—I can't make any promises about yellow nacho "cheese" or those gummy slugs you get at the movies). But when was the last time you said "ya know, I could really go for some beta-carotene and potassium right now!" I'm guessing never. It's pretty likely, though, that a bowl of fresh cantaloupe on a hot summer day looks delicious—and as a result, you eat some of those nutrients.

There are many reasons why we choose the foods we do. Good nutrition does play a role, for some people more than others. As you progress toward a vegetarian diet (and the more restrictive you decide to be on the spectrum), the more challenging it can be to get the nutrients your body needs—and with that comes the added responsibility you have to yourself to pay attention to nutrition. The other factors that play into how we eat, however, will also have a great impact on your transition to veg. Let's take a look at what those influences are and how you can work with them to make sure you're eating the most energy-boosting, beautifying, strength-building (not to mention delicious) foods at all times.

☀ **Availability:** It sounds obvious, but if a certain food is not available, you're pretty unlikely to eat it. Many low-income neighborhoods lack clean grocery stores that carry attractive, fresh produce, which is one of the reasons why people living in those areas have a harder time eating healthfully than people in higher-income areas—good-for-you food is just not easy to find.

⇨ How it impacts you: You might have the best of intentions when it comes to living life as an über-healthy veg. But if whoever does the grocery shopping in your house buys loads of steak, pork, and potato chips and few vegetables, beans, and grains, you may have a hard time following through on your intentions.

⇨ What you can do: Offer to help out with the grocery shopping or even volunteer to do it for your family. A simple trip to the supermarket or farmers' market is truly the first step in eating and can alter the foods that are available to you. By influencing what goes into your family's weekly shopping cart, you immediately impact what goes on everybody's plates and ends up in their bellies. Before you go, make a list of the foods you'd like to have in the house (see page 96, "VegHead Shopping List," for ideas)—experts say that having one increases your likelihood of coming home with nutritious foods and minimizes impulse buys (the candy display at checkout? prime impulse buy territory).

☀ **Cost:** It's no doubt that money influences how we live our lives and particularly how we eat. For many people, making decisions about what foods to buy is less about nutrition and taste and more about how much things cost. I'm never going to argue that people should max out their credit cards to buy foods they can't afford—they shouldn't. But everybody can afford to eat a more plant-based diet. The reason: the healthiest foods are basic, inexpensive ones like vegetables, beans, and whole grains. And they all just happen to be veg friendly.

⇨ How it impacts you: Many people have the misconception that it can be expensive to go veg or even to eat healthfully in general. The parental units that pay for your food may be averse to the idea for that very reason.

⇨ What you can do: Assure them that, like any other way of eating, going veg *can* be more expensive. But it doesn't have to be. If you load up on processed vegetarian foods like soy hot dogs, fake cheese, and vegan cupcakes, the cost is going to add up. If you stick with healthier whole foods (meaning items that come from nature rather than ones that have been dolled up in a factory—think carrots and celery instead of veggie chips, milk and frozen berries to blend your own smoothies with instead of premade smoothie pellets), your grocery bills are likely to decrease (see page 99 for more tips on being a "Budget Veg").

☀ **Culture:** The part of the world you live in or your family comes from plays a major role in the way you eat. If you were raised in Spain, it would be typical for you to have a big lunch at around 2:00 followed by a *siesta* or nap, a light snack at around 5:00, and a smaller meal again after 9:00. If you were raised in the United States, you probably haven't had a nap after lunch since kindergarten, and lunch is likely something small and fast like a sandwich, with dinner being your biggest meal of the day. Even within one country, there are loads of cultural differences in terms of food—I notice it all the time when I visit new cities. In places like Portland, San Francisco, and New York, veg-friendly options abound. Travel to Dallas or New Orleans, however, and meat and seafood are clearly king.

⇨ How it impacts you: The culture in your family and city will undoubtedly play a big role in how accepted it is to go veg. If you are of Indian descent, you may be used to having a plethora of meat-free options at your fingertips—many Indians are lacto vegetarians. On the other hand, families from other countries may have a hard time accepting that a meal without meat is still a meal. One great movie scene sums it up perfectly: in the film *My Big Fat Greek Wedding*, the main character tells her aunt from Greece that her fiancé is a vegetarian. "He don't eat no meat?" exclaims the auntie. "That's OK. I make lamb!" In addition to your family helping or hindering your decision, the culture of the area you live in will also impact how easy or hard it is for you to shift to a more plant-based diet.

⇨ What you can do: Well, you can't choose your relatives. But you know them better than anyone else does, and you can figure out how to best help them get used to the idea of you going veg. Maybe you have a second cousin who has been a vegetarian; point her out to your mom as a reminder that she hasn't shriveled up (yet). If you're from a culture where skipping meat is simply not accepted, you need to feel comfortable enough in your decision to agree to disagree. Work on reaching an understanding with your relatives that you won't try to change them if they won't try to change you. As for the culture of the area in which you live—you probably didn't choose that, either, unless you're college-age. If you're not in college, start researching now. Look for schools in a veg-friendly part of the country, with a culture that supports various eating choices, and put them at the top of your list (see page 147 for "Finding A Veg-Friendly College"). And in the meantime, if you're struggling to find the support system you need in a place like Hereford, TX (aka "the beef capital of the world"), look for online societies that you can be a part of—a vegetarian group through Meetup or Facebook, or the website for this book, www.smartgirlveg.com.

✳ **Positioning:** The larger environment impacts the foods you eat, as discussed above in "availability." But your immediate surroundings determine far more about the food you choose than you might imagine. How many times a day do you think you make a decision about food? Well there's breakfast, lunch, dinner, and snacks, so about four or five, right? According to Cornell University food psychologist Brian Wansink, that number is more like 250 per day. The reason why you probably underestimated is that we are completely unaware of most of these decisions. This impacts our health because we are all more likely to overeat or make choices we don't *really* mean to make when food is served in bigger portions and when snack foods are just an arm's length away (compared with food you'd have to stand up to grab a handful of).

⇨ How it impacts you: The week I stopped eating red meat, I went to a friend's bat mitzvah party. I was halfway through eating a mini hot dog before I realized I had just broken my resolution to never eat a cow again. Of course I knew that mini hot dogs had meat in them (well, sort of—who knows what's really in those things!) and I never would have walked over to a server and requested one. But when a waiter came around to my group of camp friends with a tray of hors d'oeuvres, I mindlessly grabbed a hot dog and started munching away. Those sorts of unconscious decisions can make VegHead eating extra challenging: you might grab a hamburger for lunch because it's the first thing you see when you walk into the cafeteria. But if your lunchroom offered California veggie wraps front and center, you would be more likely to choose the veggie option without even knowing you're making a choice. Of course, deciding to go veg is a very active decision. But the placement of veg-friendly options in your home, school cafeteria, and other places you eat can make veg eating feel more or less like a challenge.

⇨ What you can do: This is where that active decision thing comes in. After my mini hot dog gaffe, I never made that mistake again. The reason: not eating meat was in the forefront of my mind. I couldn't control what was offered to me, so I had to stay in charge. The next time I found myself at a party, I stayed on the dance floor instead of around the food. You can't change the positioning of foods you don't want to eat, but you *can* change your position!

☀ **Promotion:** You're too smart to be swayed by slick ad campaigns, right? We all think we are. But the reality is that fast-food companies alone spend more than $300 million on marketing aimed at teens and kids each year—the average teen sees about five fast-food ads on TV each day (and that's not counting radio, Internet, and mobile ads or advertising through Facebook, YouTube, or Twitter that often don't even feel like ads). This exposure has a huge impact on what teens eat, according to the experts who study food advertising and marketing. I actually had a summer internship once where it was my job to watch cartoons and kid movies to look for the ways they promote not-so-healthy foods. It. Was. Awesome. It was also scary to see firsthand how sneaky advertisers can be.

⇨ How it impacts you: The ads you're exposed to are sure to be influencing you to choose foods that are not so good for you as well as ones that don't match up with your VegHead instincts. Those McDonald's, KFC, and Subway promotions you see every day regularly nudge you to crave their food. And even if you know deep down their food is not for you, the constant barrage of ads you see may be undermining your efforts.

⇨ What you can do: Limit your exposure. Watching less television—or DVRing your favorite shows so you can skip over the ads—is one way to do this. Also, be careful about advertising that you opt into. When a burger joint asks you to "like" them on Facebook and promises you free fries in return, yes, you get free food—but you also give that restaurant permission to market to you directly. Be sure you know what you're getting in exchange when you "like" something on Facebook, "follow" it on Twitter, or "check in" to it on Foursquare.

※ **Taste:** In my work as a registered dietitian nutritionist and as a professional eater (it's one of my best talents), I find that this is the most important factor in the foods people choose.

If it doesn't taste good, they won't eat it. Just as you are unlikely to pick a yogurt for a snack because "boy, I could sure use 150 mg of calcium right about now," you are not going to select that yogurt if you just don't like yogurt (or you're vegan or lactose intolerant, of course).

⇨ How it impacts you: It's a sad reality—many people think that vegetarian food is boring or just plain bad. And when people perceive a food as unappetizing, they don't want to eat it. Little do they know, though, that veg food is often more flavorful and interesting than meat foods. My theory: when chefs (professional or everyday ones) take meat off the plate, they are forced to be a little more creative with vegetables, herbs, and other ingredients. And creativity in the kitchen leads to delicious meals.

⇨ What you can do: Don't be discouraged by what "people" say. The Negative Nancies who say that vegetarian food isn't good have clearly not eaten many meatless meals in their time. I'm not guaranteeing that you'll love everything, but if you keep an open mind, you will find loads of delicious veg-friendly foods. And you never know—when Nancy sees your mouth-watering meal, she may be enticed to give veggie food a second chance.

"It's not nutrition unless you eat it!"

We've looked at VegHead nutrition from the most miniscule of vitamins and minerals to the large factors that play a role in your diet. But as I like to tell my clients, "it's not nutrition unless you eat it." Getting delicious foods—that happen to meet your body's needs for health and well-being—onto your plate and into your mouth is the ultimate goal here. So let's talk food.

I want to introduce you to something called MyPlate, a healthy eating tool developed by the United States Department of Agriculture (USDA). It's really pretty simple, which is what I love about it.

In short, MyPlate encourages you to fill half of your plate with produce, one quarter with protein, and one quarter with grains. As a longtime VegHead, I was thrilled when the USDA introduced MyPlate—finally, a recommendation that puts vegetables front and center! In this country, it's not uncommon to see a meal consist of a big hunk of meat, a starchy food like potato or rice, and vegetables that seem like an afterthought (a couple of beige pieces of oversteamed broccoli or a limp iceberg lettuce salad). I love that MyPlate nudges us to put produce first.

"Hold it right there," you're thinking. "Today's lunch was veggie chili with a cornbread muffin, and I ate it from a bowl. And yesterday I ate a plain bagel on the way to school. Meals don't only come on plates!" Fair enough, my friend. Meals come in all different forms. In order for it to be useful to your life, keep in mind that MyPlate isn't a commandment, it's a guideline. Use the fundamentals behind it—one-half produce, one-quarter protein, one-quarter grains—to help shape your meals, no matter where you eat them from. That veggie chili may already come close to those ideal proportions, while the bagel leaves much room for improvement (to put it on MyPlate, cut it in half, saving one side for tomorrow, top with peanut butter, and grab a banana—easy peasy!).

Here's what you need to know about each section of MyPlate:

Produce: MyPlate separates fruits and vegetables. I combine them. Here's why—in general, people have less trouble eating fruits than they do veggies. I like to gently nudge people to add vegetables to their meals, since that's usually what they need encouragement with. Also, there are plenty of meals where you'd eat vegetables but not fruit or vice versa. My take is: fill roughly half your plate with produce, pay a little extra attention to vegetables, and it will all work out just right at the end of the day.

Protein: Ah, trusty old protein again. While other MyPlate followers can easily stick a piece of roast beef in their protein box, that may not work for you—and that just may be freaking out every adult you know. Tell them not to panic—veg sources of protein are easy to find, and since they only need to take up about one-quarter of your plate, it's simple to add them to many meals. You can fill up the protein requirement of *YourPlate* with chickpeas, lentils, black beans, tofu, edamame, or tempeh; eggs, milk, yogurt, or cottage cheese (other cheeses can be a decent source of protein, but they are often so high in fat that you're better off looking at them more as a garnish) if you're lacto-ovo; fish like tilapia or salmon and seafood like shrimp and scallops if you're pescetarian; and chicken or turkey if you're a red head.

Grains: This is an easy category for VegHeads since all grains are inherently meat-free (sometimes the way in which they're prepared can make them surprising sources of meat, though—check out Chapter 6 for more on that). The trick with grains is choosing the healthiest ones for you. In general, you want to look for whole grains—ones that have been minimally refined and still contain their outer layers that include stomach-filling, digestion-improving, heart-healthy fiber and other important nutrients. Often, whole grains are brown or beige in color—think of the difference between white rice and brown rice, and you'll know how to recognize a whole grain. Other whole grains include oats, barley, wild rice, bulgur, and farro. One detail you should keep in mind about the grains category—it also includes starchy vegetables like potatoes, sweet potatoes, and corn (did you really think I was going to OK half a plate full of mashed potatoes?!). They're super healthy for you like other types of vegetables, but higher in carbohydrates like grains, and eating too many can give you a quick energy boost followed by a major crash—so you'll want to eat them with more restraint than, say, spinach and cauliflower.

Dairy: You'll notice on the graphic of MyPlate that it includes a glass of milk, representing one serving of dairy. Obviously, this spells trouble for vegans and anyone else who chooses to not consume moo juice and other related products. Some nutrition experts argue that dairy does not deserve this sort of emphasis—there's no proof that eating a lot of dairy protects you against osteoporosis, some dairy foods are loaded with heart-unhealthy saturated fat, and the nutrients that make lowfat dairy good for you, like calcium and protein, can easily be found in other foods, they say. If you are vegan—and even if you're not, but you *are* wondering how you could possibly down a glass of milk with each meal—my advice is: don't get too hung up on dairy. A serving of tofu or a cup of cooked collard greens both have more calcium in them than a cup of milk, for instance. And the protein that dairy foods provide can also be found in beans, nuts, and other vegan foods. You're already making sure to get plenty of protein in your meals. As for the other nutrients dairy is a good source of, eat a varied, nutrient-packed diet (as discussed in Chapter 4) throughout the day as well, and you'll be just fine. Oh, and if you do include one beverage with every meal, make it water (or unsweetened seltzer or iced tea—skip the sodas and juices). It will help keep you hydrated and avoid unnecessary sugar (even the natural sugar in fruit juice isn't necessary—you're much better off eating whole fruits).

Where's the Fat?

One criticism of MyPlate is that it doesn't explicitly include any fat. Fat, in case you don't know, is an important nutrient, crucial for keeping your skin and hair vibrant, absorbing vitamins, making hormones that send messages throughout the body, and providing structure to all of your cells as well as your brain. So why isn't there a fat section on MyPlate? The simple answer is that we tend to eat fat as part of our meal rather than as a standalone item. Dressing and avocado on your salad and the fats naturally found in protein foods like tofu, fish, nuts, and eggs all count toward your fat for the day. What you need to know about this nutrient: with the exception of the omega-3s found in fish, which you read about in Chapter 4, the fats you want to eat are the plant-based ones. You're best off avoiding "solid fats" (aka solid at room temperature), which may come to you naturally as a VegHead since they're found in foods like meat, cream, and butter. They're also in veg-friendly foods like margarine, shortening, and hydrogenated oils used in many packaged foods. Instead, get your fat from plant-based sources like vegetable oils (like olive and canola), avocados, nuts, olives, and seeds.

MVP (Most VegHead Player) Grain Spotlight: Quinoa

This not-technically-a-grain grain (it's actually a seed, though experts consider it a grain since we eat it like one and it's nutritionally similar to other members of that family) is native to the Andes mountains and has had a huge increase in popularity over the last few years. People love quinoa because it cooks quickly, tastes great in a lot of different recipes, and is extra healthful—it's also naturally gluten free, making it a super food find for people who can't eat the protein found in wheat. The reason why quinoa is especially useful for VegHeads is that it's higher in protein than most other grains. A half cup of cooked quinoa has about four grams of protein, while the same amount of brown rice has around half that much. It's also one of the only plant foods that contains all of the essential amino acids your body needs (you'll remember from Chapter 4 that it's no big deal if you don't get them all in one meal, but you can think of it as an added bonus). While it will give your meal a protein boost, quinoa is still a starchy food that you should use to fill the "grain" portion of your plate rather than the "protein" one. But if you're feeling like your plate is a little light on pRotein, choosing quinoa can be an easy way to get moRe of the muscle-building, satisfying nutRient. In addition to plain old quinoa, look foR the gRain in otheR foRms like pasta, flouR, and hot ceReal to give meals an unexpected pRotein boost. And keep youR eyes open foR the not-as-populaR gRains buckwheat and amaRanth—they'Re also good souRces of pRotein that contain all nine essential amino acids.

BREAKFAST: WAKEY WAKEY EGGS (MAYBE) AND (FAKE) BAKEY

You've heard people say that breakfast is the most important meal of the day. And research shows that's actually true. Teens who eat breakfast regularly eat more healthfully overall than those who don't. They're also more likely to be at a healthy weight (people who skip breakfast tend to get super hungry and overcompensate by eating too much later in the day; doing so may also negatively impact your metabolism). One recent study found that teenage girls who skip breakfast are twice as likely to have diets low in iron and calcium (among other vitamins and minerals), which makes it an extra important meal for veg-leaning teens who are already at an extra risk for not getting enough of these nutrients into their days.

Eating breakfast impacts more than your physical health. It plays a big role in your performance at school. Students who eat breakfast are more alert in class, have an easier time remembering things they've learned, and are generally in better moods. Oh, and they also tend to score higher on tests. If that ol' sleeping with the textbook under your pillow the night before an exam trick hasn't worked for you yet, try eating breakfast instead (and a little studying probably won't hurt, either).

So explain to me why, with all of these benefits, 34 percent of girls age six to eighteen say they don't eat a morning meal. The top two reasons I hear from girls about why they don't eat breakfast are: "I'm just not hungry when I wake up," and "I have no time to eat!" Here's what you can do about both:

"I'm just not hungry."

It's hard to eat if you're not in the mood—and there's nothing wrong with listening to your body and respecting the cues it sends you. That said, there's no denying that eating breakfast regularly is a healthy habit. While I don't suggest forcing anything down your throat, here's what you can do: eat later. There's no rule that sitting down for breakfast has to be the first thing you do when you get up in the morning. Instead, wake up, take a shower, put the finishing touches on your math homework, and eat as you're ready to head out the door. Or make a habit of packing an on-the-go breakfast or mid-morning snackfast (snack/breakfast) that you can eat in an hour or whenever you're ready for it.

"I have no time."

Allow me to be blunt. If you have time to hit the snooze button even just once, you have time for breakfast. If you have time to check Facebook, you have time for breakfast. If you have time to put on makeup or dry your hair, you have time for breakfast. None of these tasks take very long, and eating breakfast doesn't have to, either. Before you go to sleep at night, make a mental note of what you plan to eat in the morning. If your breakfast of choice requires any preparation, do it before you get into bed. It may even help to get your breakfast ready to go, even if it doesn't require much work. Set an empty bowl, a spoon, and a box of cereal on the kitchen table so when you see it, you have a reminder to sit down and eat. And if you really, really cannot manage to eke a couple of minutes out of your morning routine for eating, make sure your kitchen is stocked with portable foods that you can grab and go (see below for specific suggestions).

Breakfast tends to not be the most meat-heavy meal of the day. However, depending on where you find yourself on the VegHead spectrum, there are different issues you may face in finding the right meal for your life. Here are a few considerations for the various places you may eat in the morning:

AT HOME

FOR EVERYONE:

* Keep the pantry stocked with one or two of your favorite cereals; it's hard to find an easier go-to breakfast, and research shows that people who eat breakfast cereals regularly get more nutrients in their diets overall than people who don't.
* Do your best to sit down and eat. Yes, breakfast on the go is better than no breakfast at all—but stopping for a few minutes to focus on your meal helps your brain register that you've eaten and is a smart way to energize before you start your day.

FOR VEGANS:

* Choose a nondairy milk that is fortified with calcium, vitamin D, and vitamin B12. If you're not using soymilk or a protein-fortified milk alternative, be mindful to get some protein in your breakfast from another source like nuts, seeds, or protein-rich cereal like Kashi GoLean.

AT THE SCHOOL CAFETERIA

FOR EVERYONE:

☀ You may be surprised to find that school can be a convenient place to grab a healthy breakfast. Some schools are part of the national School Breakfast Program, which means the morning meals sold must meet certain criteria determined by the government. In other cases, schools may sell à la carte options that are not held to the same standards. Either way, the options offered may not be all that veg-friendly. Look on your school district's website for breakfast menus to decide whether or not eating at school is a good option for you.

AT THE COLLEGE DINING HALL

FOR EVERYONE:

☀ The options you find at the dining hall are going to vary widely depending on your school. But reality is that even if the options are plentiful, finding time to stop at the dining hall for breakfast simply does not happen for many students, whether their first class is at 8:00 a.m. or 11:00 a.m. Instead of missing breakfast, be sure to keep some breakfast options in your dorm room. They don't have to be fancy—a jar of peanut butter and some whole wheat bread and bananas lifted from the dining hall, dry cereal and the milk of your choice (either from the campus store or dining hall—you can bring it back to your room in to-go cups), or energy bars work just fine.

☀ If you are an early riser and do manage to get to the dining hall before morning classes, great! You'll figure out quickly if your school is among those offering veg-friendly breakfasts (they can't all be the University of Puget Sound, what with its tofu and spinach scramble, or the University of California, Santa Cruz, with vegan Mexican tofu Benedict). Perhaps you've found that your dining hall has plenty of cereal options but no nondairy milk alternative, or cooks veggie omelets in the same pans they use for ham and swiss ones—and as a result, your breakfast needs are not being met. Instead of stomping off to class cranky and hungry (bad combo!), speak up about what you'd like to see changed. Dining halls are a business just like any other restaurant, and the people who run it want to see their customers happy. Make your voice heard, whether by slipping a note into the "comments" box or scheduling a meeting with the school's foodservice representatives.

AT RESTAURANTS*

FOR EVERYONE:

✺ If there's one place where breakfast means meat, it's a restaurant. If your meal comes with a side of bacon or sausage, as many breakfasts do, be sure to specify that you'd prefer yours without. And if you're not sure what a dish has in it, don't be afraid to ask—that's what your server is there for.

FOR LACTO-OVO VEGETARIANS:

✺ Eggs and breakfast out are like peas and carrots! Mickey and Minnie! Peanut butter and jelly! If you do eat eggs, it should be easy for you to find a breakfast you'd like. And if all the egg options on the menu do contain meat (like Denver omelets and eggs Benedict do), ask for an "all-veggie omelet"—the kitchen will likely be more than happy to whip you up something special with the vegetables they have on hand and any cheese you may like.

FOR VEGANS:

- ❋ Be aware that restaurant breakfast standbys pancakes and French toast usually have eggs and milk in them—and may be cooked in butter.
- ❋ Oatmeal can be a good option, but sometimes it is prepared with milk rather than water. Consult your server.

*For more on restaurant dining, see Chapter 7, Eat Out Veggie!

ON THE GO

FOR EVERYONE:

- ❋ The time to think about eating breakfast on the go is not, I repeat, not when you're already on the go. Being prepared can take your meal from an afterthought to something nutritious that you'll actually enjoy.
- ❋ It's OK if breakfast looks more like a snack than a meal, as long as you are eating something before your day really gets going.
- ❋ On-the-go ideas: Baggies of homemade trail mix (toss cereal with dried fruit and nuts); Larabars; toasted English muffin with peanut butter and banana; yogurt (Greek, regular, or soy) and a pear; a homemade smoothie in a to-go cup (see page 173 for recipes).
- ❋ If you're already out the door and haven't so much as thought about breakfast yet (fine, I forgive you), try the following stops for healthy and veg-friendly breakfast options:

⇨ Starbucks: oatmeal with nuts and dried fruit (vegan); spinach and feta breakfast wrap (lacto-ovo); veggie and Monterey Jack artisan breakfast sandwich (lacto-ovo); KIND bars (lacto-ovo); Two Moms in the Raw granola bars (vegan); fruit salad and bananas (vegan). Note: soy milk is available for all beverages and is an easy way to get some protein in.

⇨ Dunkin' Donuts: egg white veggie flatbread (lacto-ovo); Southwest veggie burrito (lacto-ovo); plain bagel with peanut butter (vegan); blueberry muffin (lacto-ovo).

⇨ Jamba Juice: Five Fruit Frenzy smoothie (vegan); Mega Mango smoothie (vegan); Strawberry Whirl smoothie (vegan); Peach Pleasure smoothie (lacto-ovo); Caribbean Passion smoothie (lacto-ovo); steel-cut oatmeal (lacto-ovo; note that while it is made with soymilk, it contains milk ingredients); fruit and yogurt parfaits (lacto-ovo).

⇨ 7-Eleven or another convenience store: bags of nuts and dried fruit (vegan); yogurt (lacto-ovo); individual cereal boxes with milk or soymilk (vegan or lacto-ovo); Clif or Luna bar (most flavors are vegan); Odwalla bars (six flavors are vegan); hard-boiled eggs (lacto-ovo); fruit salad cups or whole fruit (vegan); string cheese (lacto-ovo).

POWER LUNCH

Let's do lunch. If you're like other busy teens, you probably welcome the opportunity to take a midday break from classes, work, chores, extracurricular activities, volunteering, and the other tasks that make life so hectic. But for many teens, it can be tough to make lunch fit into their schedules, not to mention finding foods that taste good and will give them the right balance of nutrients to fuel them until that final bell rings or soccer practice is over.

Throw a dietary limitation like not eating meat into the mix, and everyone's favorite class of the day can feel like more of a hassle than a chance for reboot. Here are some of the challenges most facing the VegHeads I spoke with:

Making Time

Some schools make lunch a priority and don't schedule any classes during the lunch hour. But other schools will let students register for as many classes as they'd like, which leaves many students with a superstar high school transcript, but no lunch period. And if you're already in college, there's no such thing as "lunch period." If you have fifteen minutes between classes and a twenty-minute walk from Zombies in Popular Media (a real class at Columbia College Chicago) on one side of campus to Tree Climbing on the other (you'll find it at Cornell University), there's no way you're getting a meal in and making it to class on time.

What you can do about it: rely on the kindness of others. Don't assume that your teacher will be OK with you eating in class—it may be against the building's policy, or it can be a safety hazard in a class like Tree Climbing (or more typical classes like biology or chemistry lab). But chances are the instructor will take pity on you and approve you to eat something inconspicuous during his or her class, even if your opportunity is restricted to the first ten minutes before you've put your helmet and kneepads on.

Some not-too-smelly, not-too-noisy lunches that you can eat out of your backpack:
- A hummus sandwich with shredded carrots and lettuce
- Regular or nondairy yogurt with berries and a bag of granola
- A thermos full of soup
- Dried fruit and string cheese

Weirdo Lunchtimes

For many students who are lucky enough to have lunch scheduled into their day, the break comes at an odd time. Don't get me wrong: it's great to have time devoted to nothing but eating and socializing (OK, and finishing up French homework), but if that break comes at 9:25 in the morning, you can't exactly call it a midday meal. Same idea if your lunch period is the last class of the day—it sounds tempting to get a break before afterschool activities start up, but if you're not eating until close to when the final bell rings, you've probably gone a seven- or eight-hour stretch without any fuel. And that means you were fading fast those last few classes.

What you can do about it: you must, must, must plan ahead for a midday snack. Use your off period to eat a real meal, since you'll have time to go to the cafeteria or off campus and actually sit and enjoy your food. But if your classes go for longer than a four- or five-hour stretch without a fuel break, you're going to need a supplemental snack. Here are some lunch boosters to help you make it through your marathon o'classes:

- An energy bar—look for one without a lot of added sugar like Larabar, Pure Bar, or KIND bar.
- A small bag of nuts—pack it yourself or buy a prebagged one like Planter's NUT-rition Heart Healthy mix or Blue Diamond 100-calorie almond packs.
- A dairy or nondairy yogurt with a Baggie of granola.
- One squeeze pack of Justin's Nut Butter plus a banana or apple.

Finding Veg-friendly Lunches at School

Like breakfast, the food options schools offer during lunchtime vary widely. Public schools that participate in the national school lunch program are under no obligation to offer vegetarian meals;

however, many do because of the large number of students who prefer to eat veg. In Florida's Sarasota County Schools, cafeteria staff offer students VegHead options like veggie pita delight with hummus and veggie taco salad with red kidney beans a few days each month. And in NYC, P.S. 244 in Flushing, Queens became what is thought to be the nation's first all-veg public school cafeteria, serving dishes like braised black beans and plantains and falafel with cucumber salad. Of course, there are also schools where the best you may do is a cheese sandwich on white bread or a slice of greasy pizza (not exactly the best foods to fuel you through the afternoon, and not helpful at all if you're vegan). If your school has veg-friendly choices, you are already well aware of them. Show your appreciation by buying them regularly and telling the food-service staff how thankful you are that they are looking out for you. If veg-friendly lunches are not the norm at your school, here are some ways to improve your options:

- **Ask, ask, and then ask some more.** The people who make decisions regarding food at your school may simply not realize that there is a demand for vegetarian food. Some school foodservice operations hold regular meetings for students to voice their opinions about the cafeteria; see if your school has such meetings and ask if you can attend. Look for a suggestion box to write in requests too. And it couldn't hurt to share some resources with your school's foodservice team. The website www.pcrm.org/health/healthy-school-lunches is run by the Physicians Committee for Responsible Medicine, an organization that promotes vegan diets, and is packed with resources (like meal ideas and vendors) and rationale (like information about the financial benefits) for including more vegetarian options that can help encourage decision-makers at your school to incorporate the foods you want into your cafeteria's repertoire.

- **Move them toward Meatless Monday.** It's a lot to ask your school foodservice team to offer veg-friendly options every day. But your district's foodservice director might be more open to test-driving vegetarian food once a week—and if that goes well, you can nudge them to expand the program. Schools and universities all over the country have adopted Meatless Monday, and the response has been overwhelmingly positive. Visit www.meatlessmonday.com/meatless-monday-school-programs for more information including tool kits for K-12 schools as well as universities.

- **Supplement what's there.** If your school has a salad bar, but there's nothing but veggies on it (veggies are great, but you know that you're going to need some protein to get through the afternoon), bring a bag of chickpeas or nuts with you to enrich your school's attempt at vegetarian cuisine with the nutrients you need. Maybe your school has turkey and cheese wraps. You can get yours without turkey of course, but if cheese every day gets old (or you're vegan), toss a single-serving container of hummus in your backpack in the morning. Order your sandwich with just veggies, unwrap it, spread on some hummus, rewrap, and you've got a vegtastic lunch.

Brown Bag Burnout

The nice thing about bringing lunch to school is that you—or whoever is packing your meal—has more options available to them than whatever you'll find in the lunchroom. That doesn't mean that brown-bagging it is without issues though. "Because I was a vegetarian, my dad made me a PB & J every day for lunch for five years of grade school," said Andy, eighteen. "I haven't eaten a single PB & J since. BLEHHHHH!" When your options are even slightly limited, it's easy to get into a rut. Here are some out-of-the-bag lunch ideas to help keep things interesting (check out page 167 for recipe ideas too):

- ☼ Use a thermos to keep hot soup or chili at the right temperature until lunchtime. Kleen Kanteen makes sleek-looking BPA-free insulated thermi (that's the plural of thermos, right?) that keep liquid hot for up to six hours.

- ☼ Try a bento (lunch) box. Bento is the traditional take-out or home-packed meal in Japan that usually consists of some combination of rice, fish or meat, and vegetables, portioned in small boxes. Compartment-based lunch carriers are available here too (I like the ones by Laptop Lunches, www.laptoplunches.com), or you can use a few small Tupperware or Pyrex containers to cobble together your own. Put whatever you'd like in your boxes; just be sure it matches up with the guidelines outlined in MyPlate to ensure a balanced bento.

- ☼ Repurpose your leftovers. Sure, you can toss the remainder of last night's Asian veggie-tofu stir fry into a container and call it a day (if you're lucky enough to have access to a microwave for reheating). But how about revamping it into an Asian wrap? Simply roll into a whole wheat tortilla and you've got lunch made. Same with the Greek salad you had for dinner. Stuff into a pita and you've got a Mediterranean pocket lunch.

VEG: IT'S WHAT'S FOR DINNER

Raise your hand if you eat dinner with your family, at least a few times a week. You're not alone—about 80 percent of parents with kids age eighteen and younger say they eat dinner as a family at least four nights per week, according to a 2005 Gallup poll. Making sure to eat dinner together is one of the best things families can do. Kids who eat regularly with their parents have healthier diets, are less likely to develop eating disorders, and do better in school, according to a growing body of research on the topic. As for the parents…well, they get to spend more time with their awesome kids, which is what all moms and dads want, right?

Benefits aside, dinnertime can be a difficult time of day for those on the veggie spectrum. When you're out and about, you have the freedom to make the choices that are right for you. If Dad's making dinner, your options may be more limited. And if your family isn't super supportive, sitting around the table for some good grub and conversation may be the moment when you get the most grief over your dietary choices.

Here are a few strategies you can use to keep the peace and help adjust your family's favorite meals so you get a dinner that tastes great and gives you the nutrition you need—without making Mom's head pop off and do that spin-around-in-circles thing.

Be Polite

Your parents taught you as much, right? Awesome if you're feeling proud about your dietary choices—you should! But it's not your job to convert your family to your eating habits, just as it's not their place to get you to change. So what does being polite entail? Well, you probably shouldn't refer to the burgers on your parents' plates as "flesh" like I did for the better part of high school (thank you again, Mom and Dad, for not killing me). And you might not want to make grossed-out, "blech" faces at their meatloaf. In other words, treat their food choices with the same amount of respect you want them to give yours—even if they don't hesitate to give you a hard time. You know—be the bigger person and all. Set a good example and take comfort in knowing that if you just sit back, eat delicious, mouth-watering meals, and feel healthy and energized as a result, before long they will be asking if there are any extra black bean burgers you're willing to share.

Stay Strong in Your Stance

Does your dad ask you if you'd like some chicken, steak, or lamb—every single night? You have every right to be frustrated. But never let 'em see you sweat. Smile, say "no thank you," and then ask Dad if he'd like some extra salad. Or ask him how his day was. Or how those Red Sox are doing this year (even if it's football season). Just keep the conversation moving—and away from the topic of your diet. If you get agitated, it sends the message that you're unsure of your decision to go veg. The firmer you are in your stance and the clearer you are in your message, the less likely people will be to try and knock you down.

Pop In Your Protein

While some meals your family eats may be completely off-limits to you (you can't exactly take the ground beef out of a pot of five-alarm chili con carne), others will lend themselves to some mixing and matching. Ask whoever does the cooking to avoid mixing meat-containing ingredients with nonmeat ones, or ask them to set some pasta, veggies, and other veg-friendly items aside for you before meat is added in. Instead of eating just the pasta or rice—the trap that so many VegHeads fall into—replace one protein with another that is right for you. Here are a few simple swaps you can make to your family's meat-based meals:

- ☼ Spaghetti and meatballs
  - ⇨ Pop out...meatballs.
  - ⇨ Pop in...frozen meatless meatballs, defrosted in the microwave.
- ☼ Chicken stir fry
  - ⇨ Pop out...chicken.
  - ⇨ Pop in...cubed tofu, stir-fried in sesame oil.
- ☼ Hamburgers
  - ⇨ Pop out...beef patty.
  - ⇨ Pop in...a frozen burger that meets your needs (like Gardenburger or vegan BOCA burger).
- ☼ Roasted chicken with mashed potatoes and string beans
  - ⇨ Pop out...chicken.
  - ⇨ Pop in...white beans drizzled with olive oil and rosemary (microwave or heat on stove).
- ☼ Steak fajitas
  - ⇨ Pop out...steak.
  - ⇨ Pop in...black beans, tossed with barbecue sauce (microwave or heat on stove).

Get in the Kitchen

If Mom throws her hands up in the air saying, "I just don't know what to make anymore!" tell her you have just the suggestion (this book is full of them—check out Chapter 10 for dinner ideas that even the most stubborn meat-minded eaters will love). You see, Mom may feel like preparing a meal that makes everyone happy is her responsibility—and maybe up until now, it has been. Recognize that the decision you've made is your decision alone, and you can't expect everyone to instantly change to accommodate you. (If you do have super supportive parents who started making and eating veg-friendly dinners without batting an eyelash, great! But know that you're lucky. Not everyone has such support from the start.) Instead of making this Mom's burden, carry some of the weight along with her. In addition to sharing ideas from this book, keep your eyes open for recipes and meal ideas from newspapers, blogs, and more (check out Chapter 9 for useful resources). Oh, and the assistance you offer doesn't have to end there. Even if your parents love cooking, they will probably not mind getting a day off every now and then. Offer to make dinner for the whole family, just once, or once each week. If Mom and Dad are hesitant about eating meat-free meals, the trade-off of having dinner on the table when they get home from work may be just enough to convince them to give it a try. And no doubt, the delicious recipe you've chosen combined with your burgeoning cooking skills will make their appetites for veg grow.

Meatless Mondays at Home

In addition to your school, your household can also make the decision to start each week fresh with one meat-free day. Share the Meatless Monday website with your family so they can see some of the benefits of nixing meat one day per week. Explain that you're not trying to alter the way they eat; rather you're showing them how tasty and easy eating vegetarian can be—and wouldn't it be great to make a difference as a family by agreeing to this one small change? You can also offer to cook dinner for everyone on Mondays, to make it just a little more palatable for your parents to jump on board with this plan.

EXTRAS: SNACKS, DRINKS, DESSERTS

If you're a lacto-ovo vegetarian, extras like munchies, beverages, and sweets shouldn't cause much trouble for you—I mean, when was the last time you had a cake with meat in it? (You may want to check out Chapter 6 for surprising sources of meat-based ingredients; however, those examples are the rare exceptions.) If you're transitioning to being vegan, however, there's a lot of potential that the foods you eat may contain ingredients that you're actively trying to avoid. Here are a few tools to help you ensure that the extras you're eating are vegan-tastic:

Survey the Sweetener

In a move toward making products more natural, a number of companies are using ingredients like cane sugar, agave, and honey to sweeten foods and beverages instead of high-fructose corn syrup, which is made using a chemical process. If you avoid honey since it comes from bees, this could spell trouble for you. You may also be staying away from sugar that's been whitened by bone char. (Say what? See page 110 for more details.) Be sure to read ingredient lists for sweet foods—even if they're benign-seeming ones like iced teas and sauces—to make sure you're comfortable with all of the ingredients.

Have Some Go-tos

If your friends are chowing down on buttery chocolate chip cookies, it's reasonable that you might not crave a Baggie full of carrot sticks or apple slices. Fresh fruits and vegetables are always vegan, yes—but they may not feel like the foods you want to munch at an all-night *Twilight* marathon sleepover (of course— nutrition nerd alert here—if fruits and veggies do satisfy your snack tooth, more power to you!). If it's got to be junk, here are some PETA (People for the Ethical Treatment of Animals)- approved vegan options you'll find at mainstream grocery stores around the country:

- Oreo cookies
- Vienna Fingers
- Nutter Butter cookies
- Unfrosted Pop Tarts
- Entenmann's single-serve snack pies—cherry, lemon, and apple
- Fritos
- Lay's Classic Potato Chips
- Jolly Ranchers
- Sour Patch Kids
- Fruit by the Foot

Get Baking

Some cities have an assortment of vegan bakeries to choose from (see Chapter 7 for a sampling of sweet spots you can visit around the country). In other places, though, shopkeepers will look at you like you have three heads if you ask if any of their cookies are egg and dairy free. Regardless of where you live, however, you can turn your kitchen into a vegtastic dessert factory. Added bonus: your homemade treats will cost a lot less than professionally made vegan baked goods, which are notoriously pricey. Not to mention you get to eat cookies, muffins, and more fresh out of the oven. Check out Chapter 9 for recipe resources, along with the recipes in Chapter 10.

Vegpreneur: Nia Froome, Founder of Mamma Nia's Vegan Bakery

Think you're too young to put on an apron? As a seventeen-year-old high school student, Nia Froome had little experience baking. She had also never run a business before. But inspired by a lesson in an entrepreneurship class about cookie queen Mrs. Fields, Nia decided to develop a business plan for a vegan cookie company. While Nia is not a vegan herself, she chose to make her company vegan as a tribute to her parents who had gone vegan ten years before, when her mom was diagnosed with breast cancer. Mamma Nia's Vegan Bakery took off, with Nia eventually winning a nationwide youth entrepreneur contest that granted her a $10,000 prize and an opportunity to meet President Barack Obama at the White House, among other things. Nia's advice for veggie and other teens who are starting to experiment in the kitchen: Be persistent. "Don't be afraid of failure," she says. "You're going to mess up before you get a recipe exactly the way you want it. But it's not hard if you enjoy what you're doing."

VEGHEAD SHOPPING LIST

As you've read, eating well as a vegetarian often depends on being prepared. Making sure your kitchen is stocked with the right foods is going to determine how easy or hard your transition to veg is. And whether it's you or a parent who does the grocery shopping in your house, at some point somebody has probably thought "well, what the heck do I buy now?" This guide is designed to take the guesswork out of grocery trips. Choose your favorite foods from each category for a complete kitchen.

EVERYONE:

☀ Fresh produce (choose one or more of each, depending on your family's needs)

⇨ Salad greens: romaine lettuce, mixed greens, baby spinach, arugula

- ⇨ Leafy greens for cooking: kale, chard, spinach, escarole
- ⇨ Cruciferous vegetables: broccoli, broccoli rabe, cauliflower, brussels sprouts, red cabbage, green cabbage, napa cabbage
- ⇨ Starchy vegetables: potatoes, sweet potatoes, corn
- ⇨ Other vegetables: carrots, cucumber, tomatoes, avocados, eggplant, bell peppers, garlic, onions
- ⇨ Herbs/spices (fresh or dried): basil, parsley, rosemary
- ⇨ Fruit (vary based on season, cost, etc.): apples, pears, bananas, melon, berries, citrus

✳ Beans
- ⇨ Your favorite beans, canned or dried: chickpeas, cannellini beans, kidney beans, black beans
- ⇨ Hummus or other bean dip
- ⇨ Tofu or tempeh, if you like them

✳ Grains
- ⇨ Whole-grain pasta
- ⇨ Quinoa
- ⇨ Bread: whole wheat English muffins, sandwich thins, loaf of bread
- ⇨ Rice: brown rice, wild rice
- ⇨ Tortilla: corn or flour
- ⇨ Other grains: millet, amaranth, grits, polenta, oatmeal
- ⇨ Boxed cereal like Cheerios, Kashi GoLean, Shredded Wheat, granola, and more

✳ Dairy or dairy alternatives
- ⇨ Lowfat milk or alternative milk: soy, almond, coconut or other
- ⇨ Yogurt (recommended: Greek yogurt) or alternative

✳ Nuts/seeds
- ⇨ Whole nuts: walnuts, almonds, peanuts

- Peanut or other nut butter
- Individual packets of peanut or other nut butter
- Tahini
* Oils
  - Olive
  - Canola
* Snacks
  - Bars: Larabar, KIND bar
* Frozen
  - Amy's meals
  - Frozen fruit bars
  - Frozen vegetables
* Condiments
  - Mustard
  - Barbecue sauce
  - Ketchup

IF YOU'RE LACTO-OVO, ADD:

* Milk: lowfat, organic
* Yogurt: regular or Greek yogurt like Oikos
* Eggs: pastured or organic
* Cheese: your favorites like mozzarella, swiss, or grated parmesan

IF YOU'RE PESCETARIAN, ADD:

* Fresh fish
* Canned fish
  - Sardines
  - Salmon
  - Tuna

IF YOU'RE VEGAN, ADD:

- ❊ Nondairy milk alternative
- ❊ Nondairy yogurt
- ❊ Chia seeds/flaxseeds (for use instead of eggs in baking, see Chapter 10 for details)
- ❊ Nutritional yeast

Budget Veg

As you may have already learned, many people subscribe to the misconception that vegetarian foods are expensive. Of course, you know that cost depends on the choices you and your parents make at the grocery store. Vegetarian ingredients—vegetables, fruits, grains, beans, nuts, eggs—are not super pricey, especially when you compare them to the cost of meat (expensive, especially if you look for higher-quality conscious carnivore meat options like organic and grassfed varieties). Vegetarian products, on the other hand—veggie burgers, fake meats, soy cheese, frozen meals, coconut milk "ice cream"—can really add up, price-wise. Here are some strategies for keeping grocery costs down:

Focus on whole foods. Convenience comes at a cost. Buy foods in their least-processed state as much as possible—kitchen staples won't break the bank, while premade foods just may. Think a sack of potatoes rather than a bag of frozen roasted potato wedges—you or your parent can easily slice, toss with some oil and salt, and roast away.

Shop on sale. Pay attention to discounts offered at the grocery store, and mix it up according to what's on special. It's not important to buy the same things from week to week—in fact, it's healthier if you vary the specific foods you eat so you get a range of nutrients. If you want to buy organic fruit, don't commit to berries or bananas. Simply pick up the one that's a better value. And stock up wherever you can when you see discounts on pantry staples that won't soon go bad like pasta, sauces, and condiments.

Be a coupon queen. If there's one thing packaged food companies love, it's getting you to try their products. So while you may not see many coupons for items like carrots and milk, you're very likely to find ones for things like frozen bean and cheese burritos and meatless meats. Look for coupons in the circular that comes with the weekend newspaper, on company websites (if there's a new food you'd like to try, visit their site to see if there's a coupon you can print), on coupon apps or websites like couponmom.com, or in the newsletter that you can pick up when you enter the grocery store. Whole Foods is one grocery chain that offers loads of discounts on veg-friendly foods.

DIY it. Instead of springing for frozen veggie burgers that cost $5.00 per box, make your own for just pennies per patty. You can even prepare them ahead of time and store in aluminum foil in the freezer for the same convenience of store-bought frozen burgers. Check out Chapter 10 for one great meat-free burger recipe.

Save up for splurges. You're probably not going to figure out how to make meatless bologna at home, and that's OK. But cut costs where you can. For instance, canned beans are an inexpensive food—but dried beans are downright cheap, and the savings can really add up if you eat beans as much as some VegHeads do (it also doesn't hurt that beans you've hydrated yourself often taste a lot better than the mushy ones you'll get from a can).

Hydrating Beans

Using dried beans is super easy, saves money off your grocery bill, and makes beans taste way better (if you've never liked beans before, try them this way before you sign them off for good). There are two methods you can use:

QUICK SOAK:

Put beans in pot with double the amount of water as beans. Bring water to a boil for 2 minutes. Remove from heat and allow to soak for 1-2 hours. Drain liquid. In a pot, boil twice as much water as you have beans. Add beans and cook for 1-1.5 hours or until soft.

SLOW SOAK:

Cover beans with twice as much water and soak overnight, anywhere from 8-18 hours. Drain liquid. In a pot, boil twice as much water as you have beans. Add beans and cook for 1-1.5 hours or until soft.

What The Heck Are...*tofu, tempeh,* and *seitan?*

You've heard of tofu. But that's not the only meat mimic you'll see popping up on vegetarian menus. Here's the lowdown on these replacement products:

Tofu: Created by a process similar to the way milk is turned into cheese; this protein-rich Asian staple is available in the U.S. in several different textures—extra firm, firm, and silken—and can be used in a wide range of different ways.

Tempeh: Made from fermented soybeans, this grainy, nutty cake (you can slice it or crumble it) is rich in filling fiber as well as protein.

Seitan: Often sold as "mock duck" or "mock chicken" in Asian restaurants, this fake meat is actually made from the protein in wheat known as wheat gluten. Some vegetarians don't like it because its texture is too meaty!

.CHAPTER 6.

SNEAKY SOURCES OF MEAT, DAIRY, AND MORE

SOMETIMES, MEAT CAN BE LURKING WHERE YOU LEAST EXPECT IT.

On the surface, the "how to" part of going veg seems pretty obvious. Order the veggie burger instead of the cheeseburger. Say "neither, thanks," when the server asks whether you'd like bacon or sausage with your pancakes. You get the picture. But sometimes, meat can be lurking where you least expect it. If you're also trying to avoid dairy and eggs, your challenge becomes even greater.

Recently there was an uproar when people discovered that Starbucks was using cochineal extract, a red food dye made from crushed-up dried bugs, in its strawberry-flavored Frappuccinos (no worries if that's your favorite flavor—the coffee chain has since switched to a plant-based dye). And a bunch of years ago, frustrated vegetarians sued McDonald's for using beef flavoring in their French fries (they've since changed the formula, but look out, vegans: in a bizarre twist, they now they use milk-based ingredients to mimic the taste of beef).

So how can you tell when a food contains a stealth animal product? There are a few tricks.

❋ **Food allergy labels:** To protect people with serious food allergies, the Food and Drug Administration (FDA) requires companies to disclose any ingredients sourced from the eight most common allergens that are included in the product: milk, eggs, fish, shellfish, tree nuts, peanuts, wheat, and soybeans, either by bolding the allergenic item in the ingredients or by stating "contains eggs" or whatever it contains immediately after the ingredients list. Unfortunately, though, you're still on your own for meat—since few people are allergic to it, companies are not required to disclose when a product contains meat-sourced ingredients.

✳ **Kosher labels:** According to the Jewish dietary laws, milk and meat should not be eaten together. Many food manufacturers affix labels to their products to let consumers know if the food is kosher (meaning it meets the Jewish food regulations). They then go a step further to tell consumers if the food is meat, dairy, or *pareve*, which means that it doesn't contain any meat or dairy (so someone who keeps kosher can eat that food with either a meat-containing meal like roasted chicken, or a milk-containing one like a grilled cheese sandwich). A pareve food may still contain eggs or honey, so it doesn't mean a food is vegan. Since kosher labeling is something a company chooses to do—it's not required by the government in the same way food allergy labeling is—it doesn't necessarily mean anything if you *don't* see the label. Look for the word "pareve" on any kosher symbol to indicate the food contains neither meat nor dairy.

Of course, there are plenty of times when food labels aren't at your disposal, like at a restaurant or scoop-it-yourself candy store like Dylan's Candy Bar (a must-see if you're ever in New York!). And yes, some VegHeads take a "what I don't know won't hurt me" approach—and if you do, that's totally your business. But if you are dedicated to keeping meat or more out of your diet 100 percent of the time, here are a few surprising meat, fish, dairy, and egg sources that you should probably be on the lookout for.

SOUP

SNEAKY INGREDIENTS: MEAT, FISH, DAIRY

Even vegetable-loaded soups can be made with meat-based stock (or broth) like chicken or beef, or dairy ingredients like heavy cream or cheese. Some chain restaurants make it easy for you by labeling which soups contain meat and dairy. But if the restaurant you're eating at doesn't use labels, ask your server which soups on their menu are completely vegetarian.

VEGETARIAN PAD THAI

SNEAKY INGREDIENTS: EGGS, FISH

If you've ever eaten Thai food, you probably know what pad thai is—it's one of the cuisine's most popular dishes. In case you don't— it's a really tasty rice noodle–based dish that traditionally contains shrimp or chicken and vegetables and is garnished with lime juice and crushed peanuts, among other things. While "vegetarian" versions may use tofu in place of the chicken or shrimp, they often still contain stir-fried egg as well as fish sauce, a condiment frequently used in Thai cooking. If you are vegan, order "vegetarian pad thai, no egg or fish sauce please." Your server will be more than happy to accommodate you.

SALAD DRESSING

SNEAKY INGREDIENTS: MEAT, FISH, DAIRY, EGGS

You'd think that salad is the ultimate "safe" food when you're looking for veg-friendly meals. Well, it is—mostly. Some salad dressings can surprise you with their very unveggie ingredients. For example:

- ✸ Caesar: anchovies, eggs
- ✸ Ranch: buttermilk, eggs
- ✸ Spinach salad dressing: bacon
- ✸ Russian: eggs

FRENCH FRIES

SNEAKY INGREDIENT: MEAT, DAIRY

As you may remember in my story about how I stopped eating meat, there were years of my life when I thought french fries were a suitable vegetarian meal (do not, I repeat, do not try this at home—I am here for you to learn from my mistakes!). But before 2001, McDonald's used beef extract as an ingredient to add flavor to their fries. They abandoned this practice years ago after complaints (not to mention lawsuits) from religious and vegetarian organizations. Now, however, the iconic fast-food fries do contain some dairy—so while they're suitable for lacto-ovo vegetarians, they're not OK for vegans. Sorry, vegans. And unfortunately, McDonald's isn't the only establishment with fishy fries. They're usually safe, yes—but a trend sweeping the country has a number of chefs frying their taters in duck fat (luckily the use of dairy is pretty unusual). When in doubt, ask. And for those of you who love yourself some fries, here are a few spots you can hit up for VegHead-approved meat-free, dairy-free ones:★

- ✸ Five Guys Burgers and Fries
- ✸ Carl's Jr.

※ In-N-Out Burger
※ Burger King

*It's impossible to know what really goes on behind the scenes at any restaurant. If you wouldn't be comfortable eating fries cooked in the same oil as meat, ask your server what their establishment's policy is.

CHEESE

SNEAKY INGREDIENT: MEAT

It comes as no surprise to hear that cheese is not an animal-product-free food (thanks, Captain Obvious). But there's another ingredient in many cheeses that may upset even milk-loving vegetarians. Rennet is a collection of enzymes that is typically extracted from the stomachs of calves and used in cheese production. Some manufacturers use enzymes from vegetable sources and refer to them as vegetarian rennet. If you're icked out by the idea of stomach enzymes, there are a few ways you can make sure the cheese you eat is thoroughly lacto-ovo vegetarian:

※ Look for cheeses made with vegetable or vegetarian rennet.
※ Buy cheeses made with microbial rennet, a fungus or bacteria (yummy!) that can play the same role as rennet enzymes in cheese production.

SOY CHEESE

SNEAKY INGREDIENT: DAIRY

Confused yet? You should be. A number of "nondairy" cheeses and other products on the market like coffee creamer actually contain a dairy-derived ingredient called casein. A protein found in cow's milk, casein helps give some cheeses the texture and meltability that you expect cheese to have. Some soy- or almond-based cheeses use a touch of casein in their formulations for just that reason—nondairy cheese can kind of stink without it. (I mean, what's cheese without the capacity to melt?) Some vegans are OK with that little bit of casein in their cheese, others are not—only you can make the right decision for yourself. To make life a bit easier, if casein-containing cheeses are not for you, there are some newer completely vegan cheeses on the market. They tend not to be tops in terms of nutrition (few nondairy cheeses are)—but if you are vegan and really need a cheese fix, you may want to give these brands a try:

- Daiya (www.daiyafoods.com)
- Galaxy Nutritional Foods (www.galaxyfoods.com)
- Vegan Gourmet (www.followyourheart.com)

WORCESTERSHIRE SAUCE

SNEAKY INGREDIENT: FISH

One of the main ingredients that gives Worcestershire sauce its savory taste is anchovies. You can, however, find completely vegan versions of the sauce: Annie's Homegrown is one brand that tastes great and is available widely.

RICE

SNEAKY INGREDIENT: MEAT

So rice itself is meat-free, no doubt about that. But it's not uncommon for restaurants to cook rice in chicken broth in order to give it flavor. This is a particularly common practice in Spanish and Mexican restaurants—I was crushed a few years ago when I realized that my favorite taco joint in Boston cooked their rice in chicken broth, and my regular veggie burrito order wasn't so veggie at all (they've since started offering vegetarian rice as an option—go Anna's Taqueria!). In most cases, there's no way to know what's in your rice unless you ask. I've done some of the work for you. Here are a few national chains where you can fill your rice bowl with confidence:

* Chipotle Mexican Grill
* Moe's Southwest
* Baja Fresh

BEANS (REFRIED, BAKED, AND OTHER)

SNEAKY INGREDIENT: MEAT

Loaded with protein and other nutrients that you need to look out for when you give up meat, beans are a superstar vegetarian food. Fry them up in *lard*, however, and few would think of them as vegetarian anymore—and this is why it's important to keep in mind that at many restaurants, refried beans is code for, ahem, "cooked in lard." If you don't want pig on your plate, be sure to inquire about the ingredients used in any refried bean-containing dish. And other beans may have meat in them as well—for instance, the pinto beans at Chipotle Mexican Grill are cooked with a bit of bacon (their black beans, however, are completely veg-friendly). Baked beans are also typically made with ham or bacon, unless they're labeled "vegetarian."

What the Heck Is...*Lard?*

Lard is a fancy way of saying "pig fat." It can be used as a fat for cooking (like oil or butter) or to flavor various foods.

BAKED! LAY'S BARBECUE-FLAVORED POTATO CRISPS

SNEAKY INGREDIENT: MEAT, DAIRY

Chicken in barbecue potato chips? And meat? You may be wondering why. There are some things in life I simply cannot explain. Barbecue sauce does not typically contain meat or dairy. But these barbecue-flavored potato chips do. Buyer beware (for the record, regular Lay's barbecue chips and other barbecue-flavored chips I've looked at are perfectly veg-friendly).

SUGAR

SNEAKY INGREDIENT: MEAT

So it's not meat exactly, but much of the cane sugar in this country (about half of the sugar manufactured) is processed to its pure white color using bone char, or ground-up charred cow bones. If you want to keep animal products out of your treats, here are some bone-free sweeteners you can try instead:

- ❄ Vegan cane sugar, which uses an animal-free way to decolorize sugar
- ❄ Organic sugar, which is processed without bone char
- ❄ Beet sugar, which is processed differently than cane sugar; bone char is never used
- ❄ Try a different sweetener: turbinado, demerara, or muscovado sugars, evaporated cane juice, maple syrup, agave, molasses, honey (if you're not vegan)

CANDY

SNEAKY INGREDIENT: MEAT

In addition to the sugar issue, many types of candy also contain gelatin—a derivative of cow skin, cartilage, and bones. Sweets in particular to look out for: marshmallows, gummy bears, sour peaches and other gummy candies, many jelly beans (Jelly Belly beans are not made with gelatin, though they are coated with a mixture that contains nonvegan beeswax), Altoids, Starburst, Junior Mints. Here are some vegan-approved candies, according to PETA:

- Dum-Dum Lollipops
- Airheads
- Sour Patch Kids
- SweeTarts
- Dots
- Mike and Ikes
- Runts
- Twizzlers

CHOCOLATE

SNEAKY INGREDIENT: DAIRY

It's obvious that milk chocolate has, well, milk in it. But if you're on a dairy-free diet, you shouldn't take it for granted that other types of chocolate are automatically milkless. Many, particularly the more popular brands you'll find in most grocery stores, contain dairy-derived ingredients. If you're looking to stay away from milk, look for chocolate that contains nothing but cocoa butter, cocoa, lecithin, vanilla, and sugar.

OMEGA-3 FORTIFIED FOODS

SNEAKY INGREDIENT: FISH

You learned in Chapter 4 that the best source of super brain- and heart-healthy omega-3 fatty acids is fish. If you don't eat fish, you're limited to getting your omega-3s from other sources:

- ⚘ The less potent plant-based omega-3s
- ⚘ Supplements
- ⚘ Fortified foods

If you're avoiding fish in all forms, however, you need to be selective about which supplements and fortified foods you include in your day. Just like omega-3 supplements (which you read about in "Supplemental Evidence" on page 58), the omega-3s added to foods can come from either plant- or fish-based sources. If you're avoiding ocean animals, carefully read labels to make sure the food you're buying doesn't contain any "fishy" ingredients like sardine or anchovy oil. Flaxseed oil, soybean oil, and algal oil are all vegetarian sources of omega-3s.

VITAMIN SUPPLEMENTS

SNEAKY INGREDIENT: FISH, MEAT

If you choose to take a vitamin supplement, you already know to be on alert for fish ingredients (they're now found in some multivitamins as well as omega-3 supplements). But like candy, many vitamin supplements also contain animal-derived gelatin. Look for pills that don't contain gelatin or fish oils; you can also look for ones that are specifically labeled "vegetarian."

Non-Veg Produce? This S**t is Bananas. B-A-N-A-N-A-S.

It doesn't get more plant-based than fruits and vegetables, right? I mean, if you're eating whole foods like apples, spinach, and tomatoes, you rightfully wouldn't think to consider the possibility of them containing animal ingredients—they each only have one ingredient, of course. Apples are made of apple. Spinach...you get the picture. Unless, that is, the people who grew those foods are playing tricks on us.

At a recent chemistry conference, scientists from China showed off a spray designed to lengthen the shelf life of bananas. It doesn't sound so bad—who likes mushy, brown bananas anyway? But it turns out that one of the ingredients in the spray was chitosan, which comes from shrimp and crab shells. Not only would this be a major turnoff to many VegHeads, it's also potentially dangerous for people with seafood allergies. Luckily, this spray isn't being used as this book went to press, and scientists say they're looking for another ingredient to replace the chitosan. Even so, the story is a good reminder that it's getting harder and harder to know what's truly in the food we buy. If you want to stay in control of what you're eating, I recommend taking the following steps:

1. Read, read, read. Follow websites, Twitter feeds, and more for organizations and people that will help you stay on top of stories like this one.

2. Get to know where your food comes from. That might mean shopping at farmers' markets or buying products from smaller companies with values that match up with your own.

3. Consider organic. The more stringent regulations on organically grown produce mean that there's less of a chance your food has something sneaky going on.

.CHAPTER 7.

EAT OUT, VEGGIE!

IT'S YOUR JOB TO FIND OUT WHAT IS SAFE FOR YOU TO ORDER.

The average teenager eats at a restaurant around four times per week—more often than any other age-group. But for the average girl gone veg, restaurant meals can be complicated. So what's a VegHead to do? Here are some steps you can take to guarantee that eating out remains a tension-free, delicious, enjoyable activity for you.

BE PREPARED

Look up the restaurant you're headed to beforehand. Most menus are available online, and taking time to peruse a restaurant's offerings from the comfort of your own home makes deciding on a meal a far more relaxed experience for you (because, really, no pressure when you're sitting around a table and your entire party and the server are staring you down to make a decision already). Give yourself the space beforehand to decide on some potential choices; if you aren't sure whether certain menu items are right for you, make a mental list of questions to ask your server ("is that rice cooked in chicken broth or what?"). And if there's simply nothing for you to order except for a side salad (even after you've taken these other helpful tips into consideration), you can prepare by pre-mealing or packing a protein add-on (see below).

ASK QUESTIONS

You know from the last chapter that foods, especially ones prepared at restaurants, are not always what they appear to be. Only you can decide what's important to you when it comes to how your meal is prepared. Do you consider a food suitable as long as it doesn't have any meat in it? What about an omelet cooked on the same grill as bacon and hamburgers? There's no right answer to these queries—but once you've settled on what feels right to you, it's your job to find out what is safe for you to order. That's what the restaurant staff is there for, whether it's a five-star white-tablecloth, put-on-a-dress sort of place, or a greasy burger take-out joint. So ask away.

MAKE A "MIX AND MATCH" MEAL

There may not be an entree on the menu that suits your needs and appeals to you. But take a closer look at the sides, salads, soups, and appetizers. Two or three well-chosen smaller plates can add up to a satisfying veg-friendly meal, like a bowl of black bean soup paired with a baked potato, or a spinach and cheese quesadilla with a side of sautéed broccoli. (Just don't forget to think of MyPlate as you order—tortilla chips and onion rings do not equal a meal! But nice try!) Added bonus: if you are at all indecisive, you get more than one opportunity to choose the very best food(s) the chef has to offer!

GO OFF MENU

Look at the dishes a restaurant offers as a glimpse into their kitchen. If you know what they are making, you have a basic understanding of the ingredients that they have on hand. And if you ask nicely, the chef may be able to whip you up something special. You can always ask the open-ended "can you make me a vegetarian plate?" But my best suggestion is to stay in the driver's seat by making a specific request. For instance, a lot of restaurants make cheeseburgers but don't have a veggie burger option. If you're a cheese eater, you can ask for a grilled cheese (In-N-Out Burger, a west coast chain with legions of devoted fans, has a "secret menu" that includes just this). Be creative with what you see—chances are the chef wants to keep you happy and is willing to do something a little different. Not to mention the laws of supply and demand: if enough people demand (OK, OK, politely request) more veg-friendly options, restaurants will supply them. Why go hungry when you could use your order to help make the world a better place for others who have gone veg instead?

PACK YOUR PROTEIN

You know that eating well is about so much more than simply subtracting meat from your meal. But unfortunately, many chefs haven't gotten the memo (they probably just need to read this book—buy your favorite cook a copy!). While it would be true for a server to tell you that you can order any salad without the chicken for a vegetarian salad, what you're left with is not much of a meal. If you know that the lunch or dinner you're headed out to has a lot of "grilled chicken salad, hold the chicken" sort of options but doesn't offer much in the way of veg protein you can pop in to replace that meat with, take matters into your own hands. A server Baggie of shelled edamame or cashews can help round out a Chinese un-chicken salad (one of my personal favorite orders until I realized that lettuce, crispy noodles, and sesame dressing were *not* a filling meal); a little Tupperware with a scoop of black beans can do the same for an un-barbecue chicken ranch salad.

PRE-MEAL, IF YOU MUST

If there's really nothing for you to order (aside from maybe a side salad or plate of steamed veggies), you may want to take this some-what extreme but ultra-responsible precaution. Front-load your restaurant meal with something nutritious and filling. Even if it's something as simple as a peanut butter and jelly sandwich, it does the job of ensuring you are satiated so that you can spend a pleasant meal enjoying the company of your friends or family and munch-ing on something light rather than listening to the sad, sad sound of your stomach growling.

RESTAURANT ROULETTE

Sure you're taking a chance when you eat out. But a little uncer-tainty keeps life interesting. Of course, you can do your best to eat out at places that will have good options for you. Some parts of the world are easier places than others to be vegetarian, and the restau-rants serving their cuisines reflect that. The types of restaurants listed below are generally safe bets when it comes to eating veg. You'll still want to be on alert for hidden meat sources, and prepare yourself in the same ways you would at any other restaurant before you chow down. But choosing one of the following international cuisines is likely to provide you with more options than your aver-age meat-heavy American fare.

Chinese

With vegetables, tofu, and rice playing starring roles, American-Chinese restaurants tend to be understanding that not everyone wants meat in his or her meal. With a little research and the right questions, they can be very veg-friendly places overall. To MyPlate your Chinese meal, order a veggie dish with some tofu, cashew nuts, or egg in it; add in a side of rice, noodles, or moo shu pan-cakes, and you're good to go.

GO-TO DISHES

EVERYONE:*

✴ *Buddha's delight*: vegetables cooked in a light sauce; some-times it also includes tofu. This dish got its name because it is served on Chinese New Year to honor a Buddhist tradition that nothing living should be killed on the first day of the new year. Cool, eh?

✴ *Vegetable lo mein*: wheat noodles tossed with vegetables like broccoli, baby corn, cabbage, and water chestnuts and seasoned with soy sauce and spices.

✴ *Eggplant or broccoli with garlic sauce*: usually one or the other; choose your favorite and get a plate of veggies sautéed in a delicious sauce.

*Depending on your needs, it's wise to ask if these dishes are made with oyster sauce, chicken broth, or any other surprise ingredients.

LACTO-OVO:

✴ *Vegetable fried rice*: rice stir-fried in a wok with vegetables, soy sauce, and other seasonings. Usually contains egg as well.

✴ *Moo shu vegetables*: stir-fried cabbage, mushrooms, snow peas, and other vegetables along with egg, served with a sweet sauce and flour tortilla-like wrappers for making your own little Chinese burritos.

The World Is Your Oyster (Sauce)

Chinese dishes like lo mein and sautéed vegetables can be seasoned with oyster sauce, which comes in part from, well, oysters (surprisingly, it doesn't have a fishy taste—so it can sneak up on you).

If this doesn't fit into your chosen veg path, be sure to ask before you order—most chefs will happily omit it from any dish.

Middle Eastern

Restaurants that serve Lebanese, Turkish, or Israeli food (or items from other Middle Eastern countries) can usually make plant-based eaters very happy. Vegetables like tomatoes and eggplant, grains like rice and bulgur wheat, beans like chickpeas, and olives often in the form of olive oil are all ingredients that figure prominently in this type of food, typically enjoyed with pita or a similar flat bread. It's easy to make Middle Eastern food work on your vegged-out MyPlate. Load up on salad, have a helping of one of the bean-based dishes below, and scoop it up with slices of pita or enjoy it beside a scoop of rice.

GO-TO DISHES

EVERYONE:

- *Hummus*: you probably know this dip, which has surged in popularity in recent years—most grocery stores carry it in some form, including wacky flavors like chipotle and Buffalo style. Traditionally, it's made from chickpeas, tahini (ground sesame seeds), garlic, olive oil, lemon juice, and salt—which means it's a super source of meatless protein.
- *Baba ghanoush*: a perfect partner to hummus (they taste great stuffed into pita bread together), this dip is made from mashed eggplants, tahini, olive oil, lemon juice, and garlic.
- *Falafel*: typically served in a pita stuffed with salads and

drizzled with tahini, think of these as the original veggie burgers (or more like mini sliders—you can easily fit a few into a bread pocket or wrap). They are usually made with protein-rich chickpeas or fava beans, which are mixed with seasonings like parsley and then deep-fried.

※ *Ful medames*: protein power in a bowl. Cooked and mashed fava beans, mixed with olive oil, parsley, onion, lemon juice, olive oil, and garlic.

※ *Fattoush*: this salad is made of chopped vegetables like cucumber and tomatoes tossed with mixed greens, olive oil, and lemon juice. Just beware—this and other typical Middle Eastern salads like shepherd's salad may come sprinkled with feta cheese depending on how the restaurant serves it. If you're vegan or simply not a fan, ask for yours without.

※ *Tabbouleh*: this salad is pretty safely cheese free. Typically it's made of finely chopped parsley, tomatoes, mint, onion, and garlic tossed with bulgur, olive oil, lemon juice, and salt.

LACTO-OVO:

※ *Labne*: yogurt strained until it becomes closer in consistency to a spreadable cheese; it's usually seasoned with olive oil and Middle Eastern spices.

※ *Tzatziki or cacik*: a dip made from thick yogurt mixed with cucumber, garlic, salt, and olive oil. You can use it as a dip for other foods like fried zucchini or as a topping for bread.

※ *Spinach burek/spinach pie*: either served as an individual savory pastry or a slice from a larger one, the spinach filling is usually mixed with feta or another cheese.

Indian

Since 42 percent of the Indian population is strictly lacto–vegetarian with much of the rest somewhere on the spectrum, it makes perfect sense that Indian restaurants would be loaded with veg-friendly meal options. While Indian food can vary widely depending on region, staples generally include rice, lentils, and other beans, and spices like chili pepper, turmeric, and ginger (while people often associate Indian food with "curry powder," that actually doesn't mean much—the seasoning is a blend of spices and can involve many different flavors depending on the chef who is making it). If you're looking to MyPlate an Indian meal, a scoop of a bean-based dish alongside a bunch of vegetables and some rice or bread will strike the perfect balance.

GO-TO DISHES

EVERYONE:*

- *Dal*: a protein-packed stew typically made from some type of lentils, peas, or beans.
- *Chana masala*: this slightly sour chickpea-based dish (more protein!) is typically prepared with tomatoes, onions, and spices.
- *Baingan bharta*: made from grilled smoky eggplant that's been mashed, usually with cilantro and other seasonings.
- *Aloo gobi*: this dish is made primarily of potatoes and cauliflower flavored with other vegetables and spices like garlic, onion, ginger, and turmeric.
- *Vegetable pakora*: think of this as Indian tempura (battered and deep-fried veggies typical at Japanese restaurants). An assortment of veggies dropped in chickpea flour and fried crisp.

*If you're vegan, it's wise to ask your server if any of these dishes are prepared with ghee or other animal-based ingredients, just to be safe.

LACTO-OVO:

❋ *Naan*: this soft tandoor-baked flatbread is typically made with milk or yogurt and brushed with butter before being served.

❋ *Saag paneer*: pureed spinach or another green in a thick curry sauce and mixed with Indian farmer cheese, which has a very dry and not at all melty consistency.

❋ *Vegetable biryani*: a mix of rice and vegetables flavored with a light sauce made from yogurt, cashews, coconut, and spices like ginger, garlic, cinnamon, chili powder, and saffron.

❋ *Tandoori vegetables*: an assortment of vegetables that have been marinated in yogurt, then skewered and cooked in a tandoor, or a clay oven.

Ghee Whiz!

Different varieties of Indian cooking often rely on ghee, a special type of butter. It's not uncommon at Indian restaurants for otherwise vegetarian dishes to be prepared using ghee. As well, it's possible that veg-based dishes contain a touch of cream. If you're vegan or avoiding dairy for any other reason, take extra caution to double-check before ordering.

Considering Cross-contamination

For people who have a food allergy, cross-contamination is extremely serious business—it's what happens when teensy, tiny, even microscopic bits of one food get transferred to another food, because they've been cooked on the same surface or chopped on the same cutting board. If someone with a life-threatening, say, peanut allergy, consumes a crumb of peanut, it could mean death. The difference between being a VegHead and having a life-threatening allergy is that your way of eating is by choice. Now, that doesn't mean that cross-contamination can't also be serious business for you—the idea of eating a veggie burger cooked on the same barbecue as a bacon cheeseburger may totally gross you out, and you might be ready to do everything in your power to avoid that sort of contact. But unlike someone with an allergy, you get to decide how far to take your commitment. Since restaurant kitchens are fast-moving places, it's hard to guarantee that your veggie food hasn't been prepared using the same bowls and utensils as your dining companion's meat meal. If you would consider that to be unacceptable, ask your server about cross-contamination. Some restaurants may be willing to take precautions like preparing your meal on aluminum foil, while others may look at you like you have three heads. If cross-contamination crosses a line for you, you must be willing to do your homework—and in some cases, pass on eating out. Since every restaurant kitchen is unique, I did not take cross-contamination into consideration in the recommendations you'll find in this chapter.

Chain Reaction

While local ethnic restaurants can be a safe bet, they're not the only option when it comes to eating out and vegging out. Below are a sampling of national chain restaurants that I've found to be veg-friendly.* I've chosen vegan and lacto-ovo menu items based on the ingredients indicated on the companies' websites and with the help of some corporate spokespersons; please note that cross-contamination and changes to recipes are always a possibility. For the most up-to-date details be sure to check with individual restaurants, either through their websites or customer service representatives.

*I've included specific recommendations for lacto-ovo vegetarians and vegans, as well as highlighted the chains that are tops for conscious carnivores. If you're avoiding red meat but not white, or simply eating meat less frequently, you shouldn't have any trouble figuring out which menu choices will work best for you.

What the Heck Is...*Fast-casual?*

Most of the restaurants listed here are considered "fast-casual," a relatively new term used to describe restaurants that are not-quite sit down (usually you order the made-to-order food up front and bring it to your own table on a tray), but are a bit nicer than your traditional fast-food joint (think McDonald's or Taco Bell). Fast-casual restaurants tend to use higher-quality ingredients than fast-food places (though there's no guarantee they always do), and often you have more control over what goes into your meal compared with establishments that make everything ahead of time.

SOUPS, SALADS, AND MORE

PANERA BREAD

www.panerabread.com

The menu for this soup and sandwich chain (more than 1,600 locations in 44 states) tends to be pretty chicken heavy, but with a little research (made easy since their website lists full ingredient information) you can easily find or create a meal that suits your specific needs.

If you're lacto-ovo, try: tomato and mozzarella sandwich; Mediterranean veggie sandwich; mac and cheese; vegetarian creamy tomato soup; Greek salad.

If you're vegan, try: peanut butter and jelly on sourdough bread; vegetarian black bean soup in a cup, bowl, or sourdough bread bowl; garden vegetable soup in a cup, bowl, or sourdough bread bowl (no pesto); Mediterranean veggie sandwich on sourdough or rye (no feta).

NOODLES AND COMPANY

www.noodles.com

This chain (32 locations in 22 states) doesn't stick to one cuisine—Noodles and Company serves pasta inspired by dishes from all around the world. What makes it great for girls gone veg, however, is not the variety—it's the customization factor. Each noodle, soup, and salad option comes with the opportunity to "choose your own protein." Pick organic tofu as your protein of choice and you've got a balanced veg-friendly meal made.

If you're lacto-ovo, try: penne rosa; pesto cavatappi; pasta fresca;

whole grain Tuscan linguine; Wisconsin mac and cheese; Bangkok curry; Chinese chop salad; tomato basil bisque.

If you're vegan, try: Indonesian peanut sauté; Japanese pan noodles; Chinese chop salad (no wontons); cucumber tomato salad; tossed green side salad with balsamic vinaigrette.

SOUPLANTATION/SWEET TOMATOES
www.souplantation.com/www.sweettomatoes.com

This soup, salad, and bakery chain—basically a souped up (ha!) salad-heavy all-you-can-eat—has 126 restaurants in 15 states. You know a company is veg-friendly when their loyalty club is called "Club Veg" (if you're eighteen or older, sign up on the website to get free coupons, news about menu changes, and other promotions). When you make your own salad, you have a seemingly endless number of lacto-ovo and vegan combinations at your fingertips (both veg and vegan options are marked throughout the restaurant); meat-free and vegan soups are also available and clearly labeled.

If you're lacto-ovo, try: choose from a rotating menu of clearly labeled dishes like classic Greek salad and Irish potato leek soup.

If you're vegan, try: choose from a rotating menu of clearly labeled dishes like mandarin spinach with caramelized walnuts salad and Santa Fe black bean chili.

BURRITOS, TACOS, AND BEYOND

CHIPOTLE MEXICAN GRILL
www.chipotle.com

With nearly 1,500 locations in 43 states (and expanding rapidly), Chipotle is known for preparing natural, fresh meals to order. With a mission to change the way people think about and eat fast food, which includes finding sustainable sources for ingredients, these fast-casual spots are even a suitable option for Conscious Carnivores. All of the meat this chain serves up are "naturally raised" in a humane way, and never given hormones. Also, the sour cream comes from pasture-raised cows, as does 65 percent of the cheese (a percentage the company says it is working to increase). Note that the black beans at Chipotle are vegetarian while the pinto ones are seasoned with bacon.

If you're lacto-ovo, try: a vegetarian burrito; salad bowl with black beans; fajita burrito bowl; vegetarian tacos.

If you're vegan, try: a vegetarian burrito; fajita burrito bowl; vegetarian tacos (build yours sans cheese or sour cream, obviously).

MOE'S SOUTHWEST GRILL
www.moes.com

Like Chipotle, everything at Moe's (500 locations in 35 states) is made to order—which means you control what goes into your meal, with more than twenty toppings like tomatillo salsa and roasted corn pico de gallo to choose from. Moe's is also a top choice for Conscious Carnivores, serving cage-free chicken and grassfed beef. Oh, and they give you free chips and salsa. Nice.

If you're lacto-ovo, try: Art Vandalay burrito; Unanimous Decision taco; Super Kingpin quesadilla; Ruprict nachos; Billy Barou nachos with tofu; Close Talker salad with tofu; Personal

Trainer salad; Fat Sam or Alfredo Garcia fajitas with tofu; Tofu rice bowl.

If you're vegan, try: Art Vandalay burrito; Unanimous Decision taco; Close Talker salad with tofu southwest vinaigrette dressing; Personal Trainer salad with southwest vinaigrette dressing; Fat Sam fajitas with tofu; Alfredo Garcia fajitas with tofu; Tofu rice bowl (again, you'll want to go cheese and sour cream free).

QDOBA MEXICAN GRILL
www.qdoba.com

Qdoba (600+ locations in 44 states, DC, and Canada) also lets you customize your order—so as long as you know which ingredients to avoid and request the combination that works for you, you're good to go (plus, servers prepare meals while you watch—so you can rest easy that your meal contains exactly what you expect it to). Most of the chain's main ingredients (tortillas, rice, beans, salsas) are not made with any animal ingredients, so simply skip the ones that obviously don't jibe with your food choices. Neat tip: visit the menu section of Qdoba's website to get full nutrition information for the meal you've built yourself (my "naked" black bean, rice, grilled veggie bowl with guacamole, no dairy, provides twenty-four grams of protein and 32 percent of my daily need for iron—score!).

If you're lacto-ovo, try: grilled veggie burrito; fajita veggie burrito; tortilla soup; cheese quesadilla; three-cheese nachos; taco salad.

If you're vegan, try: grilled veggie burrito; fajita veggie burrito; tortilla soup (again, sans sour cream and cheeses).

ASIAN-INSPIRED

P.F. CHANG'S CHINA BISTRO
www.pfchangs.com

This sit-down Chinese restaurant (with 208 locations in 39 states) has a special vegetarian section on their menu. Download their iPhone and Android menu app so you can decide what to order while in the car on the way over.

If you're lacto-ovo, try: coconut curry vegetables; stir-fried eggplant; Buddha's feast; vegetarian fried rice; ma po tofu.

If you're vegan, try: Buddha's feast, steamed (order a side of edamame for some protein power).

PEI WEI ASIAN DINER
www.peiwei.com

P.F. Chang's fast-casual younger sister restaurant (they're owned by the same company) has a diverse menu featuring dishes inspired by Chinese, Korean, Japanese, Thai, and Vietnamese culinary traditions. Their menu clearly labels the items that are vegetarian—provided you order them with tofu and vegetables and not chicken or beef, that is (well, duh!).

If you're lacto-ovo, try: Japanese teriyaki; honey-seared tofu; Thai dynamite tofu; spicy Korean tofu; sweet and sour tofu; vegetable spring rolls; edamame.

If you're vegan, try: Thai dynamite tofu; edamame.

PIZZA PARTY

UNO CHICAGO GRILL
www.unos.com

While most pizza places will provide you with some decent veg-friendly options, the benefit of going to a chain like Uno (130 locations in 24 states) is that their website is completely transparent (in other words, ingredients for all menu items are listed along with nutrition information). Note that the Parmesan and Romano cheese Uno sprinkles on its pizzas are both made using animal rennet; if this is a no-no for you, simply ask for other varieties of cheese instead, which are all produced with microbial enzymes. And vegans, beware: options are somewhat limited; a meal at Uno may be the right time for you to pack a protein add-on, or pre-meal with something a bit more satiating.

If you're lacto-ovo, try: veggie burger; Tuscan pesto minestrone soup; any vegetarian pizza with the Parmesan or Romano left off.

If you're vegan, try: veggie soup; any vegetarian pizza without cheese.

CALIFORNIA PIZZA KITCHEN
www.cpk.com

The vegetarian and vegan menu on this chain's website make your job super easy. Rather than just listing off the few veg-friendly options, CPK (260+ locations in 30+ states) goes the extra mile by telling you how to alter other orders to make them just right for you. (Would you have guessed that their ranch dressing and

American cheese contain meat or fish byproducts? And that multi-grain penne has egg in it? Me neither.)

If you're lacto-ovo, try: Margherita pizza; California veggie pizza; grilled veggie sandwich; quinoa and arugula salad; four-cheese ravioli.

If you're vegan, try: Dakota smashed pea and barley soup; Tuscan hummus (ask for thin crust instead of pita); Chinese chicken salad (no chicken or wontons); quinoa and arugula salad (no cheese or champagne vinaigrette); roasted veggie salad (ask for lemon herb dressing instead of Dijon balsamic); lettuce wraps (with vegetables only); white corn guacamole and chips.

Sugar Sugar

In Chapter 6, we talked about how sugar can be a surprising source of animal-based products (bone char, specifically)—and may be a big turnoff for you, depending on how you look at things. In my research, I've found that lacto-ovo vegetarians tend not to worry too much about this, while more vegans find it unacceptable. In this section, I've done my best to make sure that foods containing bone char-whitened sugar did not wind up in the "if you're vegan, try" sections of the recommendations. Please note restaurants are always changing, and the information I got when I researched this book may not be up-to-date anymore. As always, if this is something that is a major concern to you, be sure to do your own detective work before you dine.

· CHAPTER 8 ·

VEGGIE VOYAGER

Deciding where you ultimately lie on the vegetarian spectrum is a journey. But once you've landed at your happy veggie place—be it Meatless Mondays, vegan, or anything in between—you at some point will likely find yourself on a more traditional sort of trip (you know, the kind that includes luggage and an airplane ride or long car ride). And when you do, the road is likely to present you with some challenges that are different from the ones you'll encounter at home. For starters, you're eating more meals out. You're probably also eating as a group and may have to find dining options that make different people with varying opinions happy—if the people in your family ever disagree, of course (ha!). What's more, all of this communal eating may make you feel under scrutiny more than normal.

On the positive side, however, having real preferences about the food you eat can also enhance and enrich your experiences as a world traveler. Think about it: food is one of the best ways to get to know a culture or region. And by going out of your way to find what the city you're visiting has to offer in terms of vegetarian food, you are bound to learn something new about that place. It will also guarantee you get off the beaten path—meaning that instead of going to TGI Friday's for the eight thousandth time for the same meal you could get at home, you get to try something completely unique to that corner of the world (of course, sometimes chain restaurants do come in handy; in the previous chapter you read about some easily found franchises you can always count on at home and when you travel). The best part: if you find a new food or recipe you like, you get to bring the memory home with you and do your best to recreate it—and that's one of the best souvenirs ever.

Traveling with ease on a plant-based diet depends on a few things: finding great spots to eat and pick up food, being prepared, keeping an open mind, and managing the expectations of your travel companions are the overriding themes that will ensure your happy trails. Do you have a summer vacation, weekend trip, or college tour coming up? Here are a few tips that will help you on your journey:

1. Google away. When I find out I'm going to be visiting a new city, it's not long before I'm at my computer searching "name of city" (insert actual name of city here) and "vegetarian." Your results will pull up everything from restaurant websites to blog posts of reviews to local vegetarian enthusiast websites. You may also find specific websites that may be worth checking out on their own: happycow.net includes a directory of vegetarian restaurants and health food stores around the world; CHOW.com is a general food message board where people post questions like "where can I go in Oahu with a vegetarian?" and "can you recommend vegetarian-friendly but not exclusively vegetarian restaurants in NYC?" (The site is not focused on vegetarian food at all, but is a great resource for eaters of all kinds.) I've found terrific veg-friendly restaurants this way, but also some more surprising finds—gelato di soia, or nondairy soy milk gelato in Italy, and ice cream made from nothing but bananas in Hawaii, for instance (what, you don't travel the world sampling ice cream?).

2. Find a farmers' market. In the opinion of some travelers, it's not a true visit to Philadelphia unless you've had a cheesesteak,

and it simply wouldn't be a trip to Hawaii without a pig cooked underground at a luau. In my opinion, however, some of the best local delicacies are the foods that come from the earth—foods that just happen to be veg-friendly, how convenient! For instance: I didn't think I cared much about figs until I tasted them freshly picked from a tree in Greece. And the super-sweet papaya I had on Kauai beats that creepy looking pig with an apple in its mouth any day! Stopping by a farmers' market means you'll find the most local and in-season produce the region has to offer—in other words, the best. Farmers' markets may also have other items for sale such as local delicacies like the frozen maple syrup pops I found in Montreal or artisan-made crafts like the beautiful hand-dyed yarn you'll find at the Union Square Greenmarket, where I go when I'm at home in New York. And like veg-friendly restaurants, farmers' markets are also fun places to see some local flavor on display. Many have entertainment like music or street performers and in general are great for people-watching and hobnobbing with local residents. The website www.localharvest.org will help you find farmers' markets around the United States.

3. Survey the locals. If you know someone who lives in the area you're about to visit, ask her what spots you should check out. Even if she is not a VegHead herself, she's bound to know someone who is or know of a veg-friendly restaurant because it's just plain good. And if you don't know anyone who lives in the area, enlist social media. Post a message on Facebook or Twitter—chances are, somebody will know somebody who can send you in the right direction.

4. Be open-minded and ready to ask questions. Just because a restaurant isn't a designated vegetarian one doesn't mean they

don't offer plenty of veg-friendly dishes. Scour menus for something that suits your tastes. And if you don't see anything, ask the server if they can prepare something special for you. Nobody's ever been kicked out of a restaurant for being a vegetarian and you're not going to be the first. I promise.

5. Make a grocery run. When you get settled in your hotel, ask an adult to accompany you to the nearest supermarket (if you didn't notice one on the way in, ask the concierge or look it up on a computer or smartphone). Pick up a bag full of things that will make your stay easier—depending on your needs, that might mean a carton of soy milk so you can enjoy cereal from the breakfast buffet, or a few pieces of meatless jerky for the night your family wants to hit the Texas BBQ joint. If your room has a mini-fridge, you can even stock up on items that need to be kept cool like yogurt and fresh fruit.

6. Keep protein in your purse. You're pretty much always going to find something to eat. But too often, that something may be a plate of raw or cooked vegetables and not much more. And you know that protein is crucial to feeling satisfied, and that going too long without any puts you on the fast track to general grumpiness and familial bickering. (That and forgetting your headphones. DON'T FORGET YOUR HEADPHONES!) A Baggie of salted pistachios or cashews isn't a lot to carry around, but is a godsend when you're about to eat a box of iceberg lettuce and shredded carrots for lunch at a highway rest stop. Sprinkle the nuts on top to instantly turn that weak excuse for a salad into a meal. Other protein add-ons you can keep with you, depending on your tastes and your access to a refrigerator or cooler: a small can or foil packet of salmon or tuna; an individual tub of hummus; a bag of crunchy chickpea munchies (see page 216 for

recipe); mini Babybel cheese; yogurt; vegetarian jerky like Primal Strips.

7. Stay cool. If one of your travel companions—parent, sibling, or other—decides that mealtime is an opportunity to nag you about what you're eating, gently remind them that you're on vacation too. And that means that you deserve some space from their constant commentary. Agree to disagree and to put the conversation on hold for the duration of your stay. If that doesn't work, take a deep breath, order the food you'd like to eat instead of what they think you should, and move on with confidence that you are making the right decisions for you.

So now that you're ready to take off, VegHead, here is a brief guide to some of the best vegetarian or veg-friendly spots some of the most-visited cities in this country have to offer. Since you'll most likely be traveling with family or friends, remember that compromise is key. This list is focused on restaurants that will appeal to everyone—vegetarian and vegan spots that your meat-eating relatives should love and omnivore establishments that will serve your brother a burger but won't leave you lunchless. Oh, and while dessert is usually pretty vegetarian-friendly, it's not always good to the vegans—so I've included a handful of egg- and dairy-free places where everyone in your party can enjoy a sweet treat. Bon voyage!

NEW YORK

TAIM

www.taimfalafel.com

This Middle Eastern take-out spot doesn't shout "vegetarian"—but it just happens to be (items that contain egg and milk are noted on the menu). In addition to excellent pita sandwiches like falafel, salads, and fries, you can also try a signature smoothie like date-lime-banana or design your own.

PALA
www.palapizza.com

This pizza-focused non-veg place has loads of lacto-ovo options on its regular menu. It also boasts an extensive vegan menu where dairy- and egg-avoiders can find dishes with animal-free "cheese," "sausage," and other foods they usually have to skip.

LULA'S SWEET APOTHECARY
www.lulassweetapothecary.com

This old-fashioned ice cream parlor and sweet shop is seriously newfangled—everything in the store is completely vegan. Which doesn't mean, of course, that you have to be vegan to like it. With hard-scooped flavors like cookies 'n' cream and PB & J, soft-serve ones like cake batter, and packages of animal-product-free candies and baked goods, this spot is a treat for all.

LOS ANGELES

REAL FOOD DAILY
www.realfood.com

The three locations of this totally organic and vegan spot appeal to meat-eaters and VegHeads alike with super-filling meals like their spicy BLT wrap, riso primavera, and supreme burrito. It's also a great place for celebrity sightings; it is frequented by stars like Russell Brand, Tobey Maguire, and Lea Michele.

SWINGERS DINER

www.swingersdiner.com

Cooler than the average diner, the two locations of this non-veg restaurant take care of all their customers—from greasy specials like their swinger burger to keep your meat-freak brother happy to stuffed grilled cheese (lacto-ovo) and veggie joe (their lacto-ovo or vegan version of a sloppy joe, depending on how you order it) to put a smile on your face. Save room for milkshakes and dessert—dairy- and egg-free options included.

SAN FRANCISCO

GRACIAS MADRE

www.gracias-madre.com

The location of this 100 percent vegan and organic restaurant makes it extra noticeable. In San Francisco's taqueria-heavy Mission District, Gracias Madre is surrounded by traditional Mexican restaurants that are likely to use cooking methods that place meat where you're least expecting it (like in your rice, tortillas, and beans). Vegans and vegetarians alike can eat in peace here (carnivores too, since the food rocks).

DANTE'S WEIRD FISH

www.weirdfishsf.com

A seafood restaurant that's good for VegHeads (and not just the pescetarians among us)? Call it weird—but that's what they call themselves, so they probably won't mind. This restaurant has traditional from-the-ocean fare like clam chowder and fish and chips, but it also has vegan options like "hail seitan" (a fish-free fish and chips) and simpler veg choices like veggie-based tacos. Oh, and frickles (you know, fried pickles). Who you callin' weird, weirdo?

PEPPLES DONUTS
www.pepplesdonuts.com

Even Homer Simpson wouldn't blink at these 100 percent organic and vegan donuts (though I wouldn't bother mentioning it, if you do run into Homer any time soon—what he doesn't know won't hurt him). Both the San Francisco and Oakland locations serve up finger-licking varieties like salt caramel and orange creamsicle (coffee shops around town also carry their donuts, so keep your eyes open for them).

WASHINGTON, DC

MESKEREM
www.meskeremethiopianfood.com

If you've never tasted Ethiopian food, Washington, DC, is the perfect place to do so—the city has one of the highest Ethiopian populations in the country. And while most Ethiopian restaurants offer at least some veg options, Meskerem is known for their meat-free meals. Oh and added bonus—you get to eat with your hands (scooping up saucy, vegetable-y stews with injera, a spongy yummy flat bread).

BEN'S CHILI BOWL

www.benschilibowl.com

This local landmark—a favorite among celebrities and politicians—made even bigger headlines in 2009 when soon-to-be inaugurated President Obama paid it a visit (for the record, he had a chili dog and cheese fries—but we'll forgive him). Who would expect that a spot known for its meat-heavy chili, hot dogs, and burgers is also good for the VegHeads? Ben's sells veggie chili (cheese optional), veggie dogs, and vegan burgers, as well as turkey burgers and dogs for the red-meat avoiders.

BUSBOYS AND POETS

www.busboysandpoets.com

With four locations and a diverse (not strictly veg) menu that clearly labels all vegetarian and vegan options, these hip spots—the owners think of their establishments more as "community gathering places" than restaurants—will keep everyone in your family happy. In addition to food like coconut tofu bites and omelets made from locally raised cage-free eggs (attention conscious eaters!), you may also catch some local artwork, an author reading from their latest book, or an open mic poetry night.

STICKY FINGERS SWEETS & EATS

www.stickyfingersbakery.com

This 100 percent vegan bakery serves sensational sweets along with savory foods like sandwiches and quesadillas. On the weekends, you can get brunch too, (with hard-to-find egg- and dairy-free pancakes, french toast, and more).

DENVER/BOULDER, CO

MOE'S ORIGINAL BAR-B-QUE
www.moesdenver.com

Barbecue? For vegetarians? Moe's makes it possible with melt-in-your-mouth smoked tofu. Eat it as a hearty sandwich or as a plate with delish sides like mac-n-cheese and marinated slaw (options are a little more limited if you're vegan). More traditional barbecue fare like pulled pork and Angus beef brisket will keep Meatheads happy. Oh, and one of the two Denver locations also houses a bowling alley.

THE KITCHEN (NEXT DOOR)
www.thekitchencommunity.com

This Boulder spot is not exclusively vegetarian—though you'd be hard pressed to find a restaurant that's more VegHead. The chefs at The Kitchen (Next Door) are incredibly conscious about the food they serve and the ethics according to which they run their establishment. As a result, you'll find a menu full of organic and fresh foods; the restaurant also recycles or composts most of its waste. Delicious conscious carnivore, pescetarian, lacto-ovo, and vegan options abound.

CHICAGO

THE CHICAGO DINER
www.veggiediner.com

Everything at this completely vegetarian diner can be ordered vegan, even though the flavors are "as comforting and familiar as mom used to make," with meat-mimicking meals like the BBQ Bacun Cheezeburger and the Radical Reuben. If you do go for eggs and dairy, you'll be glad to know the eco-conscious products served here are all cage-free or hormone free.

HUEY'S HOT DOGS
www.hueyschicago.com

Chicago is known for its hot dogs, and Huey's is a great place to try them whether you've gone veg or not. Meat-eating members of your party can chow down on a chili cheese dog or polish sausage while you have a veggie chili dog or a vegan beer brat.

BOSTON, MA

VEGGIE GALAXY
www.veggiegalaxy.com

Across the Charles River in Cambridge, MA (home of Harvard University and the Massachusetts Institute of Technology), this vegetarian diner and vegan bakery features vibrant twists on old favorites like the BLT (made with tempeh bacon and balsamic-roasted tomato) and egg-optional, yumminess-mandatory omelets. Don't miss the delectable desserts, topped with dee-lish coconut whipped cream.

FOMU
www.fomuicecream.com

These dairy-free, mostly coconut-milk-based ice creams will satisfy any sweet tooth, in crowd-pleasing flavors like salted caramel, cookies and cream, and peppermint chip (not to mention more out-of-the-ordinary but just as fabulous ones like Thai chili peanut and avocado).

ORLANDO, FL/WALT DISNEY WORLD

COSMIC RAY'S STARLIGHT CAFE

https://disneyworld.disney.go.com/dining/magic-kingdom/cosmic-ray-starlight-cafe

This Magic Kingdom cafeteria offers both a veggie sandwich and vegetarian burger and gets extra points from reviewers for its toppings bar that includes grilled onions and mushrooms. Just be aware that while the burger is vegan, the bun is not—if you avoid eggs and dairy, ask for yours naked.

TANGIERINE CAFE

https://disneyworld.disney.go.com/dining/epcot/tangierine-cafe

This take-out spot in the Morocco section of EPCOT's World Showcase offers a vegan platter with couscous salad, hummus, and tabbouleh.

BABYCAKES NYC

www.babycakesnyc.com

The Downtown Disney location of this all-natural bakery (the first two are in Los Angeles and, you got it, NYC) specializes in cupcakes, cookies, and other sweets that are free of common allergens: wheat, gluten, dairy, casein, and eggs—making their products completely vegan in the process. Their baked goods are so beautiful and tasty, however, you may not even notice.

ETHOS VEGAN KITCHEN

www.ethosvegankitchen.com

If your group is willing to venture out of the park, you'll find a vegan haven just north of downtown Orlando featuring hearty fare like pizzas, sheep's pie (a meat-free version of shepherd's pie), and a family-friendly weekend brunch menu.

Disney Disclaimer: Disney is not known for being super veg-friendly—however frequent fliers to the Magic Kingdom insist that "cast members" are always willing to help. Forget wishing upon a star; asking servers for veggie guidance is what it takes to make your breakfast, lunch, and dinner dreams come true.

Culinary Tourism, VegHead Style

Finding veg-friendly restaurants and other businesses is something many veg-food enthusiasts love to do when they travel. Not only do they make great food discoveries this way, but they also get the opportunity to see parts of cities they wouldn't have otherwise. There's actually a name for this sort of thing: culinary tourism, which means traveling in a way that lets you experience the foods and drinks that are unique to the region you're visiting. When you focus on the vegetarian edibles that make your destination special, there is an added bonus: you'll get a glimpse into the eco-conscious culture of that city. People who open up veg-friendly businesses tend to be extra passionate about delicious vegetarian food, sustainability, animal activism, or whatever inspired them to take that route in the first place (you don't have to agree with everything their business represents—but isn't someone who is emphatic about whatever it is they believe in so much more fun that someone who is all "whatever" about it?). And maybe I'm biased, but VegHeads tend to be extra interesting people, if I do say so myself. Finding a way to connect with excited, inspired people: now that's delicious!

Sustainable Spotlight: Grazin'

In the funky little upstate town of Hudson, NY, lies an unassuming 1950s-style diner. From the outside, it looks like a place you'd go to for convenience rather than quality—but as you enter the doorway it becomes clear that this diner is something different. As stickers on the front windows indicate, Grazin' is certified Animal Welfare Approved (AWA)—in fact, it's the first restaurant in the United States to have this distinction. AWA means that all of the meat, dairy, and eggs come from AWA-approved farms, which means it's all been humanely raised on family farms. What's more, the diner also puts a premium on supporting local businesses, with nearly everything they serve coming from farms within an eleven-mile radius.

As for the food? My conscious carnivore husband loved his lamb burger, and I ate every last bit of The Bello, Grazin's lacto-ovo portobello mushroom sandwich (it is topped with a delicious buttermilk aioli). And we both devoured the addictive

organic french fries. Warning: when we were there, Grazin'
wasn't especially vegan-friendly. If you're off dairy and eggs
and decide to go there, check out the online menu beforehand
so you can supplement accordingly.

Grazin', 717 Warren Street, Hudson, NY, 12534; 518.822.9323;
www.grazindiner.com

India's Lovin' It!

If you've fantasized about a meatless McDonald's since going
veg, I have good news for you—for the price of a ticket to
Amritsar (an all-vegetarian spiritual center for the Sikh
religion) in Northern India and 28 rupees, you can sink
your teeth into that McVeggie meal you've longed for once
and for all (technically a McAloo Tiki burger, with a spicy
potato-based patty). This store is the fast-food chain's
first all-veg store in the world, and it has plans to open a
second, also in India near a Hindu pilgrimage site (Hindus
consider cows sacred).

FINDING A VEG-FRIENDLY COLLEGE

If you're reading this book, chances are at least one of the vacations
you take in the next few years will involve going to look at universities (unless, of course, you're already post–high school—in which
case, get thee to www.smartgirlveg.com to share your secrets with
your younger fellow VegHeads!). You already know that college
is an important decision—I'm not here to stress you out about it
any more than parents and guidance counselors already have. You

didn't ask, but here's my general advice on choosing a college: there are lots of terrific ones to choose from, and whichever one you wind up at is going to be awesome. If it isn't, you can transfer. Now go easy on yourself. I'm just here to make sure you eat well!

The school you choose will have a major impact on how you nourish yourself, particularly as a plant-based eater. Remember back in Chapter 5 when we talked about how your surroundings effect how you dine? By choosing a college to attend and a new city (or midsized or rural town) to live in, you are surrounding yourself with food options—ones that will either make it easier or harder to nourish yourself. You won't starve if you go to a school like Iowa State University, deep in farm country and boasting a top-ranked meat science program (yes, there is such a thing). But it can help to find a school that is supportive of your eating preferences.

There's research to be done even before you register for classes. Turn on your computer and Google "colleges for vegetarians" or something similar. Of course, there are good veg-friendly options at university dining halls all over the country, but take a pulse to see which ones are getting the most buzz at the moment. PETA, People for the Ethical Treatment of Animals, runs a Most Vegan-Friendly College contest. Even if you're not vegan, the schools on this list provide great options for all VegHeads—and everyone else, since plant-based meals are not just healthy but delicious (I've highlighted some of the best in the "School Spotlight" boxes sprinkled throughout this chapter). While you're at it, take to websites like collegeprowler.com to get the real dirt on how accommodating schools are to veg-eaters (and of course, take all posts with a grain of salt—students on anonymous message boards can be extra grumpy). For instance, the company that runs the cafeterias at Bard College in Annandale-on-Hudson, NY, boasts that they offer two vegan protein options per meal. However, a recent graduate rates the school's food as a "D+" on the website's "student reviews" section, noting that the so-called well-rounded offerings are "ill prepared"—specifically that "vegetarian protein options are mostly fried" and that "occasionally the protein option will consist of pasta." Well then.

Once you do start doing the campus tour circuit, there are a few questions you should be asking to ensure you'll be satisfied with the veggie options your school has to offer.

School Spotlight: University of California, Santa Cruz

This school observes Meatless Monday in a big way—rather than simply offering one vegetarian option, a different dining hall starts the week out by going completely veg. It also appeals to the red heads out there with Beefless Thursdays, in an attempt to further reduce the school's carbon footprint, and Farm Fridays, dedicated to local, organic ingredients, at one dining hall per week. It also doesn't hurt that the surrounding city is a hotspot for conscious eaters of all varieties—farmers' markets, restaurants, and more abound.

What's for dinner (and breakfast and lunch) at the dining halls?

Once you do begin visiting campuses, seeing and sampling the spot where you will be eating most of your meals is up there with making sure they have a major that interests you and that the dorms aren't disaster areas. Most college tours will walk you through the freshman dining hall; I recommend taking it a step further and staying for lunch (or dinner). The salad bar might look great at a glance, but is grilled chicken the only protein option? And another thing about that ubiquitous college cafeteria salad bar—how many other options are there? This is coming from someone who subsisted on little but gigantic salads (always with chickpeas on them, thank you very much) and cheese and veggie sandwiches for the two years I lived on my college campus. No, I never went hungry. But a hot meal every once in a while would have been a welcomed change. Ask if the dining hall you're visiting offers vegetarian options for entrees, and if so how often. Do they participate in Meatless Mondays? Are soups and other hard-to-know-what's-in-them items clearly labeled to let you know if they're prepared with meat? You will survive just fine at a school that doesn't go the extra mile for veg-eaters…but life will be just a bit easier at one that does.

School Spotlight: University of Florida

A focus on sustainability has earned this school a place among PETA's Most Vegan-Friedly College Contest winners in recent years. Their Animal Activists of Alachua group hosts an annual VegFest, featuring free veg food from local restaurants, and dining halls have a "vegan corner" that regularly features balanced meat-free meals.

How are the food options around campus?

The dining hall isn't the only place you'll eat. Campus coffee shops can be super useful places to get some work done or meet up with friends between classes. If you're vegan, make sure the café offers soy milk so you can get through midterms wired on caffè mochas just like everyone else. And if the café serves food, do they have veg-friendly options? Also, pay attention to the food offerings in other areas of campus. There wasn't much for me to eat between the McDonald's, Taco Bell, and Roy Rogers at my school's student union. But hidden in the basement was this little hidden gem called the Maryland Food Co-op. Sure, it had a hippie-ish reputation, and that turned some people off. But it also had the best hummus and veggies and almond butter/apple butter/banana sandwiches anywhere on campus. OK, the only sandwiches like that on campus. They were delish, and I looked forward to days I could stop there for lunch instead of the dining hall for yet another mess of salad bar. Another trend on college campuses that is a great sign for veg-eaters is the new crop of farmers' markets that have been sprouting up across the country. The markets tend to carry not only fruits and vegetables but also locally produced foods that can be easily used by kitchen-less dorm inhabitants like cheese, breads, and prepared salads. Some markets, like the one at University of California, Davis, even accept the campus cash plan. Super fresh veggie food with the swipe of a card? Enroll me now!

School Spotlight: Cornell University

Grab lunch at this school's One World Cafe, a completely vegetarian cafe featuring many locally grown and natural foods. The surrounding town of Ithaca, NY is a haven for VegHeads with an assortment of veg-friendly eateries like the famous Moosewood Restaurant, well stocked grocery stores like the GreenStar Co-op, as well as many farmers' markets and CSA options.

Are there any veggie support or veg activist groups on campus?

If you're used to being the only VegHead in your circle of friends, finding like-minded students at college is something you can look forward to when you go off to school and meet new people. A group like University of Rochester's SAVVY (Student Association of Vegan and Vegetarian Youth) may be just the place for you to find some sense of community. Is activism part of what brought you to your veggie ways? Perhaps joining an animal rights organization like Oberlin College's OAR (Oberlin Animal Rights), an environmental group like Dartmouth College's ECO (Environmental Conservation Organization), or one devoted to improving sustainable food options like Boston College's Real Food BC would be a great way for you to find other students to protest, complain, and hang out with (you know—friends!). Or maybe you have no interest in joining one of these groups at all. But know that as a person who wants to eat good vegetarian food, it's a plus to be on a campus with active, engaged students nudging campus authorities for the same things you want. Take note of what presence such organizations have.

School Spotlight: University of Illinois

Choose this school and you'll never have to pack a protein again (well, not so long as you're eating on campus). In addition to well-marked vegetarian and vegan options, dining halls have a "vegan corner" that features soy cheese and yogurt, nutritional yeast, seeds, a dried fruit and nut mix and more so you can supplement any meal that may be lacking. You can also get out of the cereal bowl at breakfast with offerings such as soy smoothies, tofu scrambles, and meatless sausage at various cafeterias.

How's the off-campus dining scene?

You're not going to eat every meal at the dining hall (thankfully!). Chances are heading off campus with friends will become part of your regular routine. Definitely spend an afternoon exploring the area surrounding any school you're looking at, and try to eat at least one meal out to get a feel for the student hang-outs. Do they have an acceptable number of VegHead options, or do you envision four years of pre-mealing it? Can you see yourself going to these sorts of restaurants with friends? You can't see into the future but asking these questions now will help you get a feel for what you may be signing up for if you send in a tuition deposit to this school.

Where would you grocery shop?

The majority of college students will live off campus at some point during their four-year (or thereabouts) stay. Look for the places you'd go grocery shopping if you did need to supply your own kitchen, since chances are you'll be looking to do just that in a year or two. Is there a local supermarket—or do off-campus students rely on boxes of cereal and instant coffee from the nearest 7-Eleven? If the town you're exploring has a supermarket, does it carry your favorite veggie hot dogs? Not the end of the world if they don't, of course—but availability of the foods that make your life a little easier may just nudge the school up a notch in your unscientific college ranking system. Perhaps the college town you're exploring has a natural foods store or a food co-op—in which case, you may have access to even more veg-friendly groceries than you'd have at home. And don't forget those campus farmers' markets that are cropping up: they can come in handy for buying ingredients as well, a serious plus if you've got any culinary chops or ambitions.

School Spotlight: Bastyr University

One of the more unusual schools out there, the curriculum at Bastyr University focuses completely on natural health, offering degrees in fields of study like naturopathic medicine, acupuncture, and nutrition. Unsurprisingly, its dining commons emphasizes plant-based whole foods and features plenty of meat-free and conscious carnivore options. Oh, and it's open to the public, so you can visit if you're passing through the Seattle area.

Are any VegHead classes offered?

While it's not a prerequisite, finding courses that match up with your VegHead values could tip the odds in a school's favor for you. For instance, Rutgers, The State University of New Jersey offers a philosophy course called Eating Right: The Ethics of Food Choices and Food Policy. At Harvard University's Science and Cooking: From Haute Cuisine to the Science of Soft Matter, students listen to lectures from celebrity chefs who are experts in molecular gastronomy (a style of cooking that takes the chemistry of food to a new level) and participate in lab classes where they get to eat their experiments (the course is now a popular lecture series, open to the public). And at Wesleyan University, you can enroll in Ecology of Eating: Reporting From the Fields of Science and Art, a course that looks at contemporary issues in food and ends with a creative project (the environmental studies course is cross-listed in the school's dance department). And while these courses are among the more unique offerings on school schedules out there, it may be something a bit more common like a strong nutrition department that catches your interest—my experiences as a teenage

VegHead landed this journalism major in an intro to nutrition class my first semester of college, and ultimately ended in me pursing a career in the field.

·CHAPTER 9·

REALLY COOL RESOURCES

YOUR COMPUTER IS AN AMAZING
TOOL WHEN IT COMES TO
FINDING YOUR PEOPLE.

Not to be all, "back when I was your age…" but back when I was your age, it was hard to find other people in my culinary situation to connect with. None of my friends at school were VegHeads; neither was anyone I knew at camp. And without other teenage vegetarians to commiserate with in the real world (or enable me to not be the only one at the barbecue eating veggie burgers, *again*), I had very little sense of community—or that there even was a community of people like me out there. I thought I was just a little weird.

Now today, we have this amazing invention called the Internet (yes, the Internet existed when I was grappling with many of the same issues you are…but let's just say it wasn't quite what it is today). In all seriousness, your computer is an amazing tool when it comes to finding your people—vegetarians, the vampire-obsessed, cupcake fiends—whatever it is that defines you. So even if you haven't encountered other VegHeads in real time, there are a number of resources that can allow a Red Head in New Jersey to help one in Arizona figure out a kind way of explaining to Grandma for the eight-thousandth time that she doesn't want to eat her famous meatballs anymore. Another way you can use the Internet to your advantage: a quick Google search can help you track down local groups that might host events like vegetarian food fairs or dinners out at veg-friendly restaurants where you can connect with real people.★ Searching around on the Web can also help you find national organizations that provide support in the form of information to support your case for going veg, resources for getting more VegHead options at school, recipes, and more.

★Disclaimer: Never, never, never meet someone you've met on the Internet alone or in private. Busy coffee shop, diner, or mall. Friend by your side. Got it?

In addition to that newfangled Internet thing, there are a number of books, magazines, and movies that can help you arrive at your happy place on the VegHead spectrum, ensure you're well fed at all times, and give you ammunition to support your decision should difficult relatives try to get in your way.

Below, some of the top sources to help you on your journey.

CLICK THIS!

MEATLESS MONDAY
www.meatlessmonday.com

If you haven't yet, take a few minutes to check out this organization. As I've mentioned just a few times in this book, the goal of Meatless Monday is to get everyone to start each week with a meat-free day to improve their health and that of the planet. If you're just getting started, you can take a pledge to go meatless on Mondays, which may give you the accountability you need to follow through on that goal. You'll also find resources for helping your school, family, and more participate in Meatless Monday, as well as up-to-date news on plant-based diets and tons of vegetarian recipes.

VEGETARIAN RESOURCE GROUP
www.vrg.org

This nonprofit organization is dedicated to educating the public on vegetarianism. Their website is a terrific place to visit for far more detailed coverage of surprising sources of meat and animal products than I was able to cover in this book, results of the many polls the organization takes of vegetarians, information for vegetarian athletes, as well as Frequently Asked Questions for vegetarian teens, and information about a college scholarship for vegetarian high school students.

PEOPLE FOR THE ETHICAL TREATMENT OF ANIMALS (PETA)
www.peta.org

This vociferous animal rights organization speaks up against animal cruelty in all forms and is a staunch supporter of vegan diets. Depending on your views, PETA might be a bit extreme for your taste—they tend to use attention-grabbing tactics to get headlines. But if you care to, you'll learn a lot from PETA's articles on factory farming, the impacts of meat production on the environment, and more. You might also want to check out PETA2 (www.peta2.org), PETA's youth division, for fun features like their Most Vegan-Friendly College Contest and Cutest Vegetarian Alive awards.

HAPPY COW: THE HEALTHY EATING GUIDE

www.happycow.net

This database of vegetarian restaurants can help you locate a suitable spot in any corner of the world you may find yourself in, from Austin, Texas, to Zurich, Switzerland. It also includes veg-friendly stores for picking up groceries. In addition, the site has a community section where you can connect with others; message boards cover topics ranging from being a vegetarian runner to converting from vegetarian to vegan.

EATING WELL

www.eatingwell.com

The website for this magazine is not just for vegetarians; however, I love to send non-meat-eaters to it for the wide range of recipes as well as their sound nutrition advice, reasonable articles, and blog posts that can help you move toward a more plant-based diet. And since *Eating Well* is a food magazine above all, the focus always is where it should be—on the yumminess. With features like "5 Amazing Thanksgiving Entrees for Vegetarians" and "Vegetarian St. Patrick's Day Menu," you'll forget all about turkey and corned beef.

POST PUNK KITCHEN

www.theppk.com

What started as a cable access TV show about vegan cooking has morphed into a community-based website and line of sassy vegan cookbooks (*Vegan with a Vengeance* and *Veganomicon*, to name a few). Isa Chandra Moskowitz pens hearty recipes like tamale shepherd's pie and quarter pounder beet burger, as well as a blog highlighting her adventures in vegan cooking. And the very active "Forum" section houses conversations on everything from where to get a certain meatless meat product in your city to cruelty-free nail polish brands (who knew?).

MEETUP

www.meetup.com

This site has nothing to do with vegetarians at all, but can be very helpful if you are one. A network of local groups, Meetup can help you find a group of people who share your interests in your city or town who "meet up" for in-person get-togethers. When I plug in my zip code and search "vegetarian," I get a choice of more than thirty groups that meet regularly. My favorite one is called "V-Rock!," a group that sounds very VegHead in its approach and meets up for activities like dinner at a hip new pizzeria (with veg and vegan options) and a picnic at a fun park on the water—maybe I'll join them for their next event. You need to be eighteen or older to sign up for Meetup—if you're not old enough, team up with your mom or dad to join and seek out interesting groups; there may be a family meetup with your names written all over it.

THE SMART GIRL'S GUIDE TO GOING VEGETARIAN WEBSITE:

smartgirlveg.com

The online home of this book—enough said!

READ THIS!

THE OMNIVORE'S DILEMMA:
THE SECRETS BEHIND WHAT YOU EAT
By Michael Pollan

The young reader's edition of this popular adult book (the original is titled *The Omnivore's Dilemma: A Natural History of Four Meals*) takes you on an undercover journey to the supermarket, exposing what's really in the foods we all eat and how they got from field, farm, or factory to your plate. If you've ever wondered where that chicken nugget really came from or what it means when an apple is labeled "organic," this is the book for you.

CHEW ON THIS: EVERYTHING YOU DON'T
WANT TO KNOW ABOUT FAST FOOD
By Eric Schlosser and Charles Wilson

After reading this young reader's adaptation of the adult book *Fast Food Nation*, that Happy Meal you used to love may not put much of a smile on your face anymore. Schlosser takes a close look at what really goes on at the large-scale farms, slaughterhouses, and meatpacking plants that supply fast-food restaurants; he also packs the book with fascinating information about how companies target their advertising and marketing efforts directly at you, the young consumer. The best part, however, is the action steps telling you what you can do to fight against the distasteful practices you've just read about (and going vegan, while it's one approach you can take, is not the only option).

VEGETARIAN TIMES
www.vegetariantimes.com

Vegetarian and vegan is the focus of this magazine, with a website that touts "the world's largest collection of vegetarian recipes." And while meal ideas pack the magazine's beautiful pages, it's also filled with useful articles on green living and staying healthy. You don't have to be a full-time veg to enjoy this magazine; it welcomes flexitarians who are experimenting with plant-based diets as well.

VEGNEWS
www.vegnews.com

This magazine's tagline sums it up: "Vegan. Think. Eat. Thrive." *VegNews* will keep you up to date on the latest news about veganism, delicious new products, vegan recipes, interviews with veg celebrities, and more. You can also sign up for a newsletter and recipe club on their extensive website.

WATCH THIS!

FOOD, INC.
www.takepart.com/foodinc

This film exposes some hard-to-watch realities about the food industry that supplies most of what we eat here in the U.S. Do corporations and even the government put profits ahead of the health of our citizens and the environment? We're producing more food that's bigger and better than ever...but at what costs? This movie has its opinion, but it's up to you to decide whether or not you agree with what it has to say. And rather than end on a depressing note, it culminates with easy steps you can take in your life to fix the food system (if you're reading this book, you've already taken one of them—go you!).

SUPER SIZE ME

www.morganspurlock.com/super-size-me

Surprise! Fast food isn't good for you. So it's not rocket science. But how bad is it really? Filmmaker Morgan Spurlock sets out to learn just that. For thirty days, Spurlock is his own guinea pig, eating nothing but McDonald's for breakfast, lunch, dinner, and snacks. Not only does he gain nearly twenty-five pounds, Spurlock also sees his cholesterol shoot up and his liver begin to develop fatty deposits, and experiences mood swings and other unpleasant side effects. Now, does eating McDonald's every once in a while have the same impact as having it three meals a day for a month straight? Unlikely. But this movie uses his experiment to take a closer look at the influence the fast-food industry has on how we eat in this country and is an interesting story for VegHeads and meat-eaters alike.

FORKS OVER KNIVES

www.forksoverknives.com

If you're wondering how going veg can improve your health, this film will provide you with loads of compelling evidence. It highlights the research of two scientists, T. Colin Campbell and Caldwell B. Esselstyn, Jr., whose research at esteemed institutions Cornell University and the Cleveland Clinic respectively have concluded that diseases like heart disease, type 2 diabetes, and certain types of cancer can be prevented or even reversed by eating a plant-based diet. Because of its focus on diseases that many adults struggle with, *Forks Over Knives* may be the perfect film to share with parents and grandparents who have questioned your decision to move toward a plant-based diet.

VEGUCATED
www.getvegucated.com

Have you ever wondered what it would be like to just go "cold Tofurky" and give up all animal products? This documentary makes an experiment of just that: the filmmakers track three meat- and cheese-loving New Yorkers who pledge to go completely vegan for six weeks. Their experiences living in the real world and dealing with skeptical relatives may sound familiar to a lot of VegHeads. And their education into the meat and dairy industries will teach you a few things that may inform your own decisions about what you eat.

.CHAPTER 10.

GET COOKIN', VEGHEAD STYLE

IF MOM IS STRUGGLING TO FIND
MEALS THAT EVERYONE WILL LOVE,
THIS CHAPTER WILL MAKE HER DAY.

The one question unassuming people never fail to ask a new vegetarian is: "So, if you don't eat meat, what *do* you eat?" The real answer: everything! Anyone who thinks that veggie cuisine is bland and lacking in options has probably never gone a meal without something that had a face. Think of the array of flavor-packed foods that are animal free: garlic, jalapeño pepper, lemon, cinnamon, peanut butter, maple syrup, not to mention every fruit and vegetable that you could possibly name. If anything, recipes that let these tongue-tickling ingredients be the stars shine on your plate even more than ones that have them play a supporting role to chicken and beef.

But, you're the one who decided to go veg...you probably already know all of this, don't you? The goal of this chapter is to give you some ideas so you can impress your friends and family with just how delicious meat- and/or dairy-free food can be. The recipes can be made by you or an adult—if Mom is struggling to find meals that everyone will love, this chapter will make her day.

All of my recipes are designed to meet the needs of VegHeads anywhere on the spectrum. All are at minimum lacto-ovo vegetarian. At the top, we'll use icons to indicate what the recipe is free of, so you can easily scan for the recipes that best appeal to you. And if one does contain dairy or eggs, I'll give you some simple swaps at the bottom so you can "veganize it." I've also included hints on making recipes gluten free, in case that is something that you or someone in your family has a need for (note: gluten is generally only a problem for people who have an allergy or intolerance to it).

Now, get cooking, VegHead!★

★The nutrition information was calculated using Nutrihand and is based on each original recipe before making any adjustments to "veganize it" or make it gluten-free.

Cooking 101

Before you get started in the kitchen, it is helpful to know what some basic words you'll come across in recipes mean. Here's a simple guide to some of the culinary terms you'll see most often:

Boil: Heat a liquid until bubbles break the surface.

Broil: Cook food directly under or above heat source; typically broiling happens in a full-sized or toaster oven. It can also be done using a barbecue.

Chop: Cut food into bite-sized or smaller pieces using a knife or cleaver.

Dice: Cut food with a knife into tiny cubes; about one-eighth to one-quarter inch in size.

Mince: Cut food into very small pieces using a knife. Pieces are smaller than chopped or diced pieces.

Preheat: Heat beforehand; usually refers to reaching a specific temperature in an oven.

Sauté: Cook food quickly over moderate heat in a sauté pan or skillet using a small amount of oil.

Simmer: Cook food in liquid at a low temperature; tiny bubbles should begin to form at the surface.

Stir fry: Cook food in a small amount of fat over high heat, stirring constantly.

Dear Veggie:

So exciting—I just got accepted to a summer foreign exchange program in England. I can't wait. But there is one thing I'm nervous about. I stopped eating meat and fish last year. I hate the idea of eating meat, but I don't want to cause trouble for my host family who will feed me breakfast and dinner five days a week. Also, I don't want these strangers to think I'm crazy! Should I just deal with it and eat meat for the summer?

Sincerely,
Reconsidering in Racine

Dear Reconsidering,

First things first—giving up meat is a lifestyle choice, and it doesn't say anything about your insanity level. If you're crazy, it has nothing to do with your food choices (har har). Now that we've gotten that out of the way, I don't think you should alter your diet preferences just because you will be a guest. Chances are your host family will be understanding about your VegHeadiness—and being up front about it will help them get to know who you are, which they are likely excited to do. Just be sure to mention the fact that you don't eat meat to them in an email before you arrive to avoid any unnecessary awkwardness. Tell them that you are flexible otherwise (you are, aren't you?) and super psyched to get to know them and to sample British cuisine. And be a gracious guest. I recommend at least trying everything they offer you that's not meat—travel is all about new experiences, including edible ones!

Bon voyage!
VEGGIE

MORNING MADNESS BREAKFASTS

BIG BANANA PEANUT BUTTER BREAKFAST COOKIE

Cookies for breakfast? Absolutely, when they're this nutritionist-approved cookie. This is the perfect breakfast for days when you think you have no time to eat. Grab one on the way out the door and you'll be the envy of all the kids in homeroom.

MAKES 6 COOKIES

1 large banana, mashed

½ cup natural peanut butter, crunchy

¼ cup maple syrup

½ teaspoon vanilla extract

1 cup rolled oats★

½ cup whole wheat flour★

½ cup unsweetened coconut flakes

¼ teaspoon baking soda

¼ teaspoon salt

1 teaspoon ground cinnamon

½ teaspoon ground nutmeg

Preheat oven to 375°F and line a cookie sheet with parchment paper. Mash the banana well in bowl. Add the peanut butter, maple syrup, and vanilla extract, and mix. In another bowl, combine the oats, whole wheat flour, coconut, baking soda, salt, cinnamon, and nutmeg. Stir the oat mixture into banana mixture until well combined (use your hands!). Roll about ¼ cup of batter into a ball and flatten slightly onto cookie sheet. Lay each cookie 3 inches apart. Bake for 12 to 15 minutes, or until lightly browned on the bottom; allow to cool for at least 15 minutes before eating.

*To make this recipe gluten free, use gluten-free oats and gluten-free baking mix.

Per serving: 350 calories, 7 g fiber, 12 g protein, 3.5 g iron, 2.6 g zinc, 77 mg calcium, 0 mcg vitamin B12, 0 IU vitamin D, 11 g choline, 0 g omega 3s

APPLE CINNAMON POWER BOWL

Hot cereal can be a super cool breakfast (see page 183 for "Choose Your Own Adventure Hot Cereal" ideas). But you'll turn up the heat—and start your day super satisfied and energized—with this protein-packed quinoa-based breakfast bowl.

Tip

Make a big batch of this on Sunday night. Multiply the amount of each ingredient by five and refrigerate what you've made. Voilà—breakfast for the week! Scoop out one bowl's worth and microwave each morning.

½ cup almond milk
¼ cup uncooked quinoa, rinsed
½ apple, chopped
1 tablespoon brown sugar
½ teaspoon cinnamon
Pinch of salt
2 tablespoons chopped walnuts

In a small saucepan, bring the milk to a simmer. Add the quinoa. Return to simmer and then reduce heat to low. Add the chopped apple and cover; cook for about 15 to 20 minutes or until liquid is mostly absorbed. Stir in the brown sugar, cinnamon, and salt and simmer uncovered until mixture thickens. Pour into bowl and top with chopped walnuts.

Per serving: 370 calories, 7 g fiber, 9 g protein, 2.8 g iron, 1.8 g zinc, 211 mg calcium, 0 mcg vitamin B12, 0 IU vitamin D, 39 g choline, .02 g omega 3s

FIGNANA SMOOTHIE

This sweet smoothie is a good source of iron and calcium, two nutrients that most every teenage girl, veg or not, could use to up her intake of. Blend up this recipe for one or double it to share with a friend.

Makes 1 serving

1 medium banana, frozen

3 large dried figs, stems removed and soaked in water for at least 30 minutes

1 cup plain lowfat yogurt

½ cup 1 percent milk

2 teaspoons blackstrap molasses

Place all ingredients in blender and blend on high until smooth.

Per serving: 390 calories, 6 g fiber, 18 g protein, 3.2 g iron, .8 g zinc, 371 mg calcium, .57 mcg vitamin B12, 59 IU vitamin D, 37 g choline, 0 g omega 3s

Veganize it: Replace vanilla yogurt and milk with nondairy substitutes such as soy, coconut, or almond yogurt and milks.

Dear Veggie,

My family always has a big Fourth of July barbecue. But nobody ever remembers that I'm vegan, and I wind up eating potato chips and watermelon for dinner. Is it rude if I ask my mom to pick up a box of veggie burgers to bring with us so I can eat too?

Sincerely,
Hungry Heather

Dear Heather,

It's not rude at all. With so many food preferences in every family—Grandpa can't have salt, Aunt Peggy's off carbs again, and Cousin Jake is still in that grilled cheese for breakfast, lunch, and dinner phase—it can be hard to keep track of who's eating what. Ask Mom or Dad to pick up a box of your favorite veggie burgers (thanks parents!). Head straight for the grillmaster and say: "Hey, these are my favorites. I thought you guys might like them too. Just save one for me!" Now, on to more important questions. Ketchup or mustard?

God bless America!
VEGGIE

SCRAMBLED N'EGGS

This completely animal-free scramble dish is good enough for all VegHeads, not to mention your meat-eating friends as well. Serve with a side of home fries or toast and a couple of slices of fruit for a spectacular Sunday brunch.

MAKES 4 SERVINGS

2 tablespoons olive oil
2 cloves garlic, crushed and minced
¼ cup minced red bell pepper

14 ounces extra-firm tofu, drained and crumbled
(use your hands!)
½ teaspoon turmeric
½ teaspoon salt
1 teaspoon minced chives
2 cups baby spinach
1 avocado, sliced

In a medium pan, sauté the garlic and pepper in olive oil on medium heat for about 2 minutes. Add the crumbled tofu, turmeric, salt, and chives, and toss until mixture is evenly yellow in color. Cook for about 2 minutes and add the spinach leaves on top. Cover with lid for about 3 minutes so spinach begins to wilt. Remove lid, mix into tofu, and cook for another 5 to 10 minutes. Toss in the avocado slices and season with salt and pepper to taste.

Per serving: 180 calories, 3 g fiber, 9 g protein, 2.5 g iron, .88 g zinc, 66 mg calcium, 0 mcg vitamin B12, 0 IU vitamin D, 6 g choline, .04 g omega 3s

CRUNCHY GRANOLA, MY WAY

So what if some people assume that just because you've gone veg, you're also a hippie? Once you've had super-addictive granola fresh out of the oven, you may not mind the association. Mix and match your favorite ingredients below for your personalized recipe—just be sure to include some nuts or seeds for protein. Layered in a parfait (see below), or in a Baggie on the way to school, you'll never be happier to be called "crunchy granola."

MAKES 8 SERVINGS

3 cups rolled oats★

½ cup unsweetened, dried coconut flakes

½ teaspoon salt

¼ cup virgin coconut oil

½ cup maple syrup

¼ teaspoon vanilla extract

¾ cup dried fruit of your choice (chopped if pieces are large): figs, apricots, raisins, cherries, cranberries, apples.

1 cup total nuts or seeds of your choice: walnuts, almonds, peanuts, pecans, sesame seeds, pumpkin seeds, cashews, sunflower seeds.

Preheat the oven to 250°F. In one bowl, combine the oats, coconut, and salt. In another bowl, combine the maple syrup and vanilla. Stir liquid mixture into oat mixture. Spread onto two baking sheets and place in oven. Bake for about 40 to 45 minutes, stirring every 10 minutes, until mixture is evenly browned. Remove from oven and let cool on baking sheet. Mix in fruit and nuts and seeds. Store in an airtight container for up to a month.

Per serving: 530 calories, 9 g fiber, 15 g protein, 3.8 g iron, .8 g zinc, 206 mg calcium, 0 mcg vitamin B12, 0 IU vitamin D, 26 g choline, 0 g omega 3s

★To make this recipe gluten free, use gluten-free oats.

Make it Parfait*

For a fancy-looking, but super easy breakfast, all you need is some cereal (granola or any other type, store-bought or home-made), yogurt, sliced fruit, and a glass. Follow these steps:

1. Put some cereal in the glass.
2. Top with some yogurt.
3. Top with some fruit.
4. Repeat until you've reached the top of the glass.
   *That's French for "perfect"

VEG MCMUFFIN

A plant-based fast-food style breakfast sandwich? For you, anything! This savory breakfast is great for mornings when you have a little more time to cook. Of course, if someone is willing to make it for you, this sammy is an easy grab-and-go that you can take on the road.

Makes 1 serving

1 teaspoon canola oil

1 egg

1 English muffin★

½ teaspoon butter

1 slice Swiss cheese

1 ¼-inch slice tomato

Coat a small Pyrex cup with canola oil. Crack an egg inside the cup and microwave on high for 30 seconds. Remove from microwave;

flip the egg and microwave for another 20 seconds (warning: all microwaves are different and you'll want to experiment to figure out what timing and power works best for yours). Toast English muffin and spread with butter or substitute. Place cheese on bottom half of English muffin, top with egg, tomato slice, and top of English muffin.

Veganize it: Use ¼ avocado, sliced, instead of cheese, Earth Balance spread instead of butter, and a ½-inch slice of tofu, cut into a circle shape, sprinkled with nutritional yeast and pan-fried on both sides until lightly browned instead of egg.
★To make this recipe gluten free, use a gluten-free English muffin.

Per serving: 385 calories, 2 g fiber, 21 g protein, 3.5 g iron, 2.7 g zinc, 352 mg calcium, 1.52 mcg vitamin B12, 58.61 IU vitamin D, 172 g choline, .38 g omega 3s

PERFECT FOR EVERYONE PANCAKES

Pancakes don't seem like a veg-unfriendly food, as long as you skip the side of bacon. But if you or someone you care about is avoiding eggs and dairy, most pancakes are out of the question. These flap-jacks are good for everybody—they use chia seeds, which means they contain heart-healthy omega-3 fatty acids; plus they just happen to be vegan (but you'd never know if I hadn't just told you).

MAKES 4 SERVINGS

½ cup all-purpose flour★
½ cup whole wheat pastry flour★
2 tablespoons sugar
2 teaspoons baking powder
½ teaspoon salt
1 cup soy milk
1 "chia egg" (see instructions below)
2 tablespoons canola oil
Extra oil for cooking

In a small bowl, mix together both flours, sugar, baking powder, and salt. In a medium bowl, whisk together the soy milk, chia egg, and canola oil. Add the dry mixture to wet, and stir until just mixed. Heat a large nonstick skillet over medium heat, and spread a thin layer of oil on pan. Spoon 2 to 3 tablespoons of batter onto skillet for each pancake and cook until small bubbles begin to form, about 1 to 2 minutes. Flip and cook on the opposite side until lightly browned. Repeat with remainder of batter—you may need to add water to thin the batter the longer it sits.

★To make it gluten free, use gluten-free baking mix instead of all-purpose and whole wheat pastry flours.

Per serving: 266 calories, 5 g fiber, 7 g protein, 2.5 g iron, .8 g zinc, 238 mg calcium, 0 mcg vitamin B12, 0 IU vitamin D, 21 g choline, 1.7 g omega 3s

Personalized Pancakes

Mix any combination of these ingredients into pancake batter before cooking to create your own unique flapjacks: sliced banana, chocolate chips, shredded coconut, blueberries, walnuts, pecans, canned pumpkin, honey, fake bacon bits, peanut butter chips, chocolate-hazelnut spread.

Egg Substitute

For baking and other recipes like pancakes, you can use chia seeds or flaxseeds to mimic the properties of egg. Place one tablespoon of chia seeds (whole or ground) or ground flaxseed in three tablespoons of water. Allow the mixture to sit for about 10 minutes, until the seeds absorb all of the water and reach a raw egg-like texture.

MEET ME IN THE MORNING OATMEAL

No time to think about breakfast when you're racing to get ready for school? Then take a few minutes before you brush your teeth and hit the hay to throw together a quick morning meal. You'll be so glad you did!

MAKES 1 SERVING

$^1/_3$ cup rolled oats

$^1/_3$ cup lowfat milk (or use nondairy)

$^1/_3$ cup lowfat plain yogurt (or use nondairy)

1 tablespoon chia seeds

Place all four ingredients in a bowl. Mix, and refrigerate overnight. In the morning, remove from fridge and season to taste. Berries, nuts, dried fruit, and spices like cinnamon and nutmeg all make fantastic toppings.

Per serving (using dairy milk and yogurt): 423 calories, 16 g fiber, 20 g protein, 4.7 g iron, 3.4 g zinc, 438 mg calcium, .38 mcg vitamin B12, 39 IU vitamin D, 14 g choline, 5.05 g omega 3s

Dear Veggie,

I've been a vegetarian for six months, and all my friends act like it's some kind of joke. I don't know any other kids in my school who don't eat meat. I like my friends, but it would be great to get to know some other people who are off meat like me (and who won't make fun of me!). How can I find other vegetarian teens if there aren't any at my school?

From,
Lonely Lindsay

Dear Lindsay,

First of all, that's really not cool that your friends make fun of you. A little harmless joking is fine, of course, but maybe it would help to have a heart-to-heart with some more understanding members of your crowd to let them know that their jabs actually do get to

you. *Of course, even if your meat-eating friends do become more supportive, it would still be nice to know some vegetarians too. It's possible that there are some at your school you don't know about. Why not start an afterschool VegHead club? You can share veg food along with your experiences going meatless. If that's not your style, get on the Internet—it will help you find vegetarians you have lots in common with, even if you're the only one in a hundred-mile radius. The website for this book, www.smartgirlveg.com is one place where you can connect with other teens just like you.*

Happy friend making!
VEGGIE

CHOOSE YOUR OWN ADVENTURE HOT CEREAL

Oatmeal is just one of many hot cereal options that will start your day on the right food. Have you ever tried rice cereal? What about buckwheat or millet? Well, what are you waiting for?! Aside from there being a huge variety of cereals to try, there are an endless number of ways you can flavor them up. Try mixing and matching some of the following whole grains with toppings and seasonings to create the breakfast that is just right for you.

Makes 1 serving

(each category is optional, except for the cereal!)

1 Start with a cereal grain	**2** Add milk (cook grain in the milk, or add to it later)
• Oatmeal • Quinoa • Buckwheat • Millet • Brown rice	• Lowfat milk • Soy milk • Rice milk • Almond milk • Coconut milk
3 Mix in produce	**4** Top with spices and extras
• Nuts: almonds, walnuts, cashews, pistachios, etc • Sliced banana • Seeds: sesame, sunflower, pumpkin • Berries: strawberries, raspberries, blueberries • Nut butters: peanut butter, almond butter • Dried fruit: raisins, cranberries, apricots • Egg • Frozen peas, baby spinach	• Sweet spices: cinnamon, nutmeg, pumpkin pie spice • Savory spices: ground pepper, rosemary, oregano • Grated parmesan cheese • Ground flaxseed • Sweetener: sugar, brown sugar, maple syrup, honey • Greek yogurt

Try these combos:

Pumpkin pie: Cook millet in almond milk, mix with walnuts and a spoonful of canned pumpkin, top with pumpkin pie spice and maple syrup.

Savory breakfast bowl: Mix cooked, hot quinoa with frozen peas, top with a fried egg, and sprinkle with grated parmesan cheese and ground pepper.

Spoon PBJ: Prepare oatmeal with lowfat milk, mix in a scoop of peanut butter, some raisins, and sprinkle with cinnamon.

Berry nutty: Heat prepared buckwheat, and mix with soy milk. Mix in pistachios, strawberries and blueberries, and top with a sprinkle of ground flaxseed and brown sugar.

Egg? In Breakfast Cereal?

Indeed! If you're an egg-eating VegHead, adding one to your morning hot cereal can be a super easy and yummy way to supercharge your breakfast. As you know, eggs add protein—the nutrient that helps sustain your energy to power you through those pre-lunch classes. You can fry or poach the egg and serve it on top of your cereal if you're in the mood for something savory. But you can also whisk it into the grains to create a creamy, pudding-like effect (trust me, it's really good!). Here's how:

1. Prepare your cereal (oatmeal, farina, cream of wheat, cream of rice, etc.) in a small saucepan on the stove, according to package directions.
2. As cereal is simmering, crack an egg in a small bowl. Mix well using a wire whisk.

3. When cereal is almost as thick as you'd like it, add a tablespoon of hot cereal to the egg. Whisk well. Slowly pour egg into saucepan, whisking vigorously. Cook until cereal is bubbling.

4. Season as you'd like: a little bit of vanilla or almond extract, a touch of sugar, and nutmeg or cinnamon are all delicious.

POWER LUNCHES

MUCHO MAC 'N' CHEESE

You'll never eat mac 'n' cheese out of a box again after you see how easy it is to make this kicked-up fancy mac. And everyone in your family will love our grown-up twist on this kid comfort-food favorite.

Makes 4 to 6 servings

8 ounces whole wheat elbows, shells, or rotini★
16-ounce package frozen broccoli and cauliflower blend
3 tablespoons olive oil
3 tablespoons flour★
1 cup 1 percent milk
¼ teaspoon nutmeg
¼ teaspoon freshly ground pepper
½ teaspoon salt
1 cup shredded cheddar cheese, sharp
1 (5.3-ounce) container nonfat Greek yogurt

Prepare the pasta according to package directions. Meanwhile, defrost the frozen veggies in microwave. In a saucepan, whisk the oil and flour over medium heat until a thick paste forms. Add the milk, nutmeg, pepper, and salt, and whisk until mixture comes to a boil and is slightly thickened. Stir in the cheese and yogurt and simmer. Drain pasta and vegetables and add to saucepan; stir until coated with cheese sauce. Serve immediately.

Veganize it: Replace regular milk and yogurt with unsweetened nondairy milk and So Delicious Greek yogurt (plain); replace cheese with ½ cup nutritional yeast and 1 tablespoon tomato paste. ★To make this recipe gluten free, use gluten-free pasta instead of whole wheat and cornstarch instead of flour.

Per serving (4 servings): 490 calories, 8 g fiber, 22 g protein, 3.2 g iron, 1.9 g zinc, 339 mg calcium, 0 mcg vitamin B12, 25 IU vitamin D, 24 g choline, 0 g omega 3s

RAINBOW SANDWICH

Why would you eat white-on-white turkey on a roll when you could put a spectrum of colors and delicious flavors between bread instead (not to mention loads of vitamins and minerals)?

MAKES 1 SERVING

2 slices whole wheat or sprouted grain bread
¼ avocado, mashed
2 thin tomato slices
1 small carrot, shredded
¼ yellow squash, sliced into thin rounds
2 leaves romaine lettuce

1 small peeled and steamed beet (like the ones sold by Melissa's),
   sliced into thin rounds
1 slice Havarti cheese

Toast the bread if desired. Spread half of the avocado mash on one side of each slice of bread. Top one slice of the avocado-topped bread with tomato, carrot, squash, romaine, beet, and cheese. Top with the second slice of bread, avocado side down.

Veganize it: Replace Havarti cheese with nondairy cheese or 2 tablespoons of hummus.
*To make this recipe gluten free, use gluten-free bread.

Per serving: 363 calories, 11 g fiber, 15 g protein, 1.3 g iron, .79 g zinc, 245 mg calcium, 0 mcg vitamin B12, 0 IU vitamin D, 19.5 g choline, .06 g omega 3s

MEDITERRANEAN PITA POCKET

This fresh and tasty sandwich is super easy to throw together. You can also put the ingredients on a plate, slice the pita into sixths, and dip away.

MAKES 1 SERVING

1 7-inch pita bread
¼ cup hummus
½ small cucumber, chopped (½ inch rounds and then in quarters)

1 small tomato, chopped

2 tablespoons chopped onion

2 tablespoons chopped parsley

5 black pitted olives, cut in half

Slice the pita bread in half. Stuff each pita half with hummus. In a bowl, toss together the cucumber, tomato, onion, parsley, and olives. Add the vegetable mixture to pita.

*To make this recipe gluten free, make a sandwich using gluten-free bread or a wrap using a gluten-free tortilla (you may need to slice the vegetables instead of chopping them).

Per serving: 351 calories, 9 g fiber, 13 g protein, 4.9 g iron, 2.3 g zinc, 162 mg calcium, 0 mcg vitamin B12, 0 IU vitamin D, 20 g choline, 0 g omega 3s

---

Dear Veggie,

I really want to go veg, but I'm worried that I'll get tired of eating the same things again and again. I'm not much of a cook, and I don't have money for expensive ingredients. Should I even bother trying to be a vegetarian?

From,
Bothered by Boredom

Dear Bothered,

I'm going to give you a challenge. The next time you are in a grocery store, pull out a pen and paper. Jot down every food you

see that does not have meat in it. Stay until you've written down every vegetarian food in the store. Kidding! You'd never leave! Point is—there are loads and loads of non-meat foods out there. Anyone, vegetarian or not, can get into a rut by eating the same foods over and over again. In fact, I find that non-meat-eaters tend to eat an even more diverse diet than meatheads. So don't be scared away. And check out the resources in Chapter 9 for magazines and websites that will give you loads of meal ideas.

Love,
VEGGIE

ASIAN CHOPPED CRUNCHY SALAD

Salads like this one typically have chicken at the center. But there's no reason why non-meat-eaters shouldn't get in on the deliciousness. Edamame, cashews, sesame seeds, and a whole lot of crunch round out this chickenless salad to make it a veg-tastic meal. Double, triple, quadruple, or more to make enough to share with friends.

MAKES 1 SERVING

DRESSING
2 teaspoons olive oil
2 teaspoons toasted sesame oil
2 teaspoons rice wine vinegar
2 teaspoons honey or agave nectar
Pinch of salt

SALAD

3 cups chopped romaine lettuce

½ red bell pepper, sliced into strips

¼ cup chopped snow pea pods

½ cup shelled edamame, boiled or microwaved according to
package directions

2 tablespoons roasted salted cashew pieces

½ orange, peeled, segmented, and cut into bite-sized pieces

1 tablespoon chopped scallions

2 tablespoons chopped water chestnuts

1 teaspoon sesame seeds

¼ cup crispy wonton noodles★

In a small bowl, whisk together the dressing ingredients. In a
medium bowl, toss together the lettuce, red pepper, pea pods,
edamame, cashews, orange slices, scallions, and water chestnuts.
Distribute into serving bowl, and drizzle with dressing to taste.
Garnish with sesame seeds and wonton noodles.

★To make it gluten free, replace wonton noodles with crumbled
rice crackers like the ones by KA-ME.

Per serving: 648 calories, 13 g fiber, 18 g protein, 6.6 g iron, 3.3 g
zinc, 196 mg calcium, 0 mcg vitamin B12, 0 IU vitamin D, 86 g
choline, .07 g omega 3s

LEAN, GREEN,★ BLACK BEAN SOUP

If you can master the art of the thermos lunch, bean-based soups
are perfect for midday meals at school. The warmth will comfort

you after a long morning of pop quizzes, note-taking, and teachers rambling, and the filling combo of fiber and protein will keep you energized through your afternoon classes.

MAKES 6 SERVINGS

1 tablespoon canola oil

1 medium onion, chopped

1 small red bell pepper, chopped

1 teaspoon pimentón (also called smoked Spanish paprika)

½ teaspoon cumin

1 (15-ounce) can chopped tomatoes

2 (15-ounce) cans of black beans, drained and rinsed

2 cups vegetable broth

¼ teaspoon salt

½ lime, sliced into 4 pieces

In a large pot, heat the oil. Sauté the onion and red pepper until soft, 3 to 5 minutes. Add the pimentón and cumin, and sauté for one minute. Add the tomatoes, beans, vegetable broth, and salt, and simmer on low heat for about 10 minutes. Puree the contents of the pot using an immersion or regular blender (leave some unblended if you'd like your soup to have some pieces in it). Pour into bowls and drizzle with lime juice.

Eat soup on its own, or sprinkle with any of these optional toppings: chopped avocado, diced red onion, chopped cilantro, shredded cheddar cheese, sour cream, crumbled tortilla chips.

*Green as in earth-friendly, that is.

Per serving: 545 calories, 24 g fiber, 32 g protein, 12.9 g iron, 8.2 g zinc, 318 mg calcium, 0 mcg vitamin B12, 0 IU vitamin D, 158 g choline, .14 g omega 3s

What the Heck is...*Pimentón?*

Also known as smoked Spanish paprika, this spice adds a meaty, almost bacony flavor to dishes and is a super smart flavor-boosting ingredient to have in your bag of vegetarian culinary tricks. You'll find it alongside other spices in the "herbs and spices" section of your supermarket.

VERY VEGGIE CHILI

Some chili recipes are loaded with ground beef or turkey. But all-veg chili is so hearty, you won't miss the meat—and neither will your friends and family (especially with a recipe like this one that uses a lot of spices to impart an extra savory flavor). This one tastes especially great with a side of corn bread.

MAKES 6 SERVINGS

2 tablespoons olive oil
1 large onion, chopped
2 cloves garlic, crushed and minced
1 green bell pepper, chopped
2 large portobello mushrooms, chopped

2 tablespoons chili powder

1 tablespoon cumin

1 teaspoon pimentón (smoked Spanish paprika)

1 (15-ounce) can red kidney beans, drained and rinsed

1 (15-ounce) can black beans, drained and rinsed

1 (15-ounce) can pinto beans, drained and rinsed

1 cup frozen corn kernels

1 (28-ounce) can crushed tomatoes

¾ teaspoon salt

In a medium pot, heat the olive oil over medium heat. Add the onion, garlic, bell pepper, and mushrooms, and sauté until vegetables are tender and liquid has cooked out, about 15 minutes. Add the spices—chili powder, cumin, pimentón—and mix well, and cook until fragrant, about a minute. Add the red, black, and pinto beans, corn kernels, and crushed tomatoes and salt, and stir. When the chili begins to bubble, reduce heat to a medium simmer and cook until thick, about 30 to 40 minutes.

Per serving: 328 calories, 17 g fiber, 16 g protein, 5.8 g iron, 2 g zinc, 146 mg calcium, 0 mcg vitamin B12, 2.8 IU vitamin D, 75 g choline, .07 g omega 3s

POWER PEANUT BUTTER NOODLES

Good old peanut butter has long been the center of many a vegetarian lunch. And for good reason—it's inexpensive, packed with protein, and of course, delicious. But PB on pasta—and served cold or at room temperature, no less? Not quite as common. Sorry jelly—PB's got a new sidekick. Get your forks ready!

MAKES 4 SERVING

1 (8-ounce) package buckwheat soba noodles★

1 clove garlic, crushed

½ inch slice ginger, peeled

½ cup natural peanut butter, no salt added

⅔ cup warm water

2 tablespoons tamari★

1 tablespoon toasted sesame oil

1 tablespoon lime juice

1 ½ tablespoons maple syrup

¼ teaspoon red pepper flakes

2 cups julienned vegetables of your choice: cucumbers, carrots,
    zucchini, red bell pepper

¼ cup chopped scallions

¼ cup salted peanuts

Prepare the noodles according to package directions. In the meantime, place the garlic, ginger, peanut butter, water, tamari, sesame oil, lime juice, syrup or molasses, and red pepper flakes in food processor, and pulse until smooth. Toss the drained noodles with peanut sauce; add the julienned vegetables and distribute into bowls. Garnish each bowl with scallions and peanuts. Enjoy warm or refrigerate for tomorrow's lunch.

★To make it gluten free, be sure to use 100 percent buckwheat soba noodles or replace the soba with rice noodles; also replace tamari with wheat-free tamari.

Per serving: 529 calories, 5 g fiber, 21 g protein, 3.4 g iron, 2.7 g zinc, 83 mg calcium, 0 mcg vitamin B12, 0 IU vitamin D, 39 g choline, .02 g omega 3s

NOT'CHO REGULAR TACO SALAD

The fun thing about this salad is you can mix and match ingredients to your liking—and the preferences of the people around you. So if your eating companion simply cannot imagine taco salad without meat in it, it's cool. She can sauté some ground beef or turkey and pop in her own protein. (Though she's totally going to be jealous of yours. Just saying.)

MAKES 4 SERVINGS

2 tablespoons canola oil

1 medium onion, chopped

1 (15-ounce) can chopped tomatoes, drained

1 (15-ounce) can kidney beans, drained and rinsed

2 cups prepared quinoa

1 teaspoon cumin

1 teaspoon chili powder

¼ teaspoon salt

8 cups romaine lettuce, chopped

1 avocado, chopped

1 cup crushed tortilla chips

½ cup shredded Monterey Jack cheese

In a medium skillet, heat the oil over a medium flame. Cook the onion until translucent. Add the cumin and chili powder and sauté for one minute. Add the tomatoes and beans and cook for 2 to 3 minutes. Add the quinoa and salt, and mix well. Evenly distribute the lettuce into four bowls, and top with equal amounts of quinoa mixture, avocado pieces, tortilla chips, and shredded cheese.

Veganize it: Replace cheese with nutritional yeast or vegan cheese.

Per serving: 499 calories, 16 g fiber, 21 g protein, 5.5 g iron, 2.6 g zinc, 151 mg calcium, 0 mcg vitamin B12, 0 IU vitamin D, 43 g choline, .36 g omega 3s

LUNCH IS JUST A PICNIC

Just because you're not eating on a blanket in a grassy field doesn't mean you can't do lunch picnic-style—in fact, these "piece it together" lunches are well-suited to school cafeterias and even classroom desks, if you have no choice but to eat and learn at the same time. Mix and match the following items to create your perfect picnic lunch.

(DIY!)

MAKES 1 SERVING

1 Choose 2 vegetables

- 1/2 cup baby carrots
- 3 stalks celery, sliced into sticks
- 1 red bell pepper, sliced into sticks
- 1 small cucumber, sliced into rounds
- 1 cup jicama slices
- 1 cup broccoli or cauliflower florets, raw or steamed

2 Choose 1 protein

- Container of Greek yogurt or soy yogurt
- 2 Laughing Cow cheeses or string cheese stick
- 1 portable container hummus (about 1/4 cup)
- 1 squeeze packet peanut butter (about 2 tablespoons) or 1/4 cup nuts of your choice (almonds, pistachios, walnuts, etc.)
- 1 to 2 hard-boiled eggs
- 1 cup steamed edamame, in shells

3 Choose 1 carbohydrate

- 1/2 cup cereal or granola
- 3/4 cup whole grain crackers
- One medium pita, sliced into triangles
- One medium corn or flour tortilla
- 3 cups popcorn or 1/2 cup pretzels
- 2/3 cup dry cereal

4 Choose 1 fruit

- One medium apple
- One medium pear
- One medium banana
- 3/4 cup red or green grapes
- One large orange or 3 clementines
- 3/4 cup melon chunks

WINNER DINNERS

VREUBEN

This veggie Reuben sandwich is just as messy and fun-to-eat as the traditional meat-containing one—not to mention super delicious. Get your napkins ready!

Makes 4 servings

¼ cup apple cider vinegar

2 tablespoons tamari★

¼ teaspoon freshly cracked black pepper

3 large portobello mushrooms, sliced into thin, wide sheets about the thickness of deli meat

3 tablespoons olive oil

1 medium onion, sliced into rounds (about 1/8 inch thick)

2 cups baby spinach leaves

8 slices rye bread★

4 slices Swiss cheese

1 cup sauerkraut, drained well

¼ cup Russian dressing

Whisk together the apple cider vinegar, tamari, and pepper. Pour on top of the mushroom slices and marinate for at least 15 minutes. Meanwhile, in a saucepan, heat one tablespoon of oil. Sauté the onions until brown. Add the spinach until wilted. Set the mixture aside. In another tablespoon of oil, sauté the mushrooms until soft and set aside. In a clean pan, add 1 teaspoon of olive oil and 2 slices of bread. Top each slice with 1 piece of cheese, 1 to 2 slices of mushroom, ¼ cup of sauerkraut, 1 tablespoon of Russian dressing, and ¼ of the onion/spinach mixture. Cook until the bread is browned and cheese melted. Top with an additional piece of bread and flip sandwich; cook until the second slice of bread is browned lightly. Repeat with the remaining two sandwiches. Cut the sandwiches in half and serve.

Veganize it: Replace regular cheese with vegan cheese or thin slices of avocado; mix up your own vegan dressing: 2 tablespoons Vegenaise, 1 tablespoon ketchup, 1 teaspoon relish.
★To make it gluten free, use gluten-free bread and wheat-free tamari.

Per serving: 460 calories, 7 g fiber, 17 g protein, 3.9 g iron, 2.5 g zinc, 317 mg calcium, 1 mcg vitamin B12, 0 IU vitamin D, 37 g choline, 0 g omega 3s

UNSTUFFED PEPPERS

Are you a fan of peppers but not the "stuff"? Try these veg-friendly peppers. Stuffed with quinoa instead of meat and simmered in tomato sauce, they are still rich and hearty enough to be a soothing dinner your whole family will love.

MAKES 4 SERVINGS

1 cup uncooked quinoa, rinsed
1 tablespoon + 2 tablespoons olive oil

½ teaspoon salt

1 medium onion, chopped

1 garlic clove, crushed and chopped

1 medium zucchini, chopped into cubes

2 large carrots, chopped into ¼ inch rounds and then quartered

½ teaspoon dried thyme

¼ teaspoon black pepper

2 to 3 cups tomato sauce

4 large red or green peppers, tops cut off and seeds removed

¼ cup pine nuts, toasted

¼ cup chopped parsley

Heat one tablespoon of oil in a saucepan over a medium-high flame and add drained quinoa. Cook for about one minute, stirring and allowing liquid to evaporate. Add 2 cups of water and salt, and bring to a boil. Lower heat, cover pan, and cook until liquid is absorbed (about 15 to 20 minutes). Turn off heat, and let quinoa sit, covered, for five minutes.

Meanwhile, in a skillet, sauté the onion in remaining 2 tablespoons of oil over medium heat until translucent (about 5 minutes). Add the garlic, zucchini, carrot, thyme, and pepper and sauté until soft, about 10 minutes. Combine the mixture with cooked quinoa. In a large pot, bring the tomato sauce to a simmer. Stuff each pepper with quinoa/vegetable mixture. Stand each pepper upright in pot; tomato sauce should be to at least half the height of the pepper. Cover pan with tight-fitting lid and cook on low for about 45 minutes, or until pepper is soft.

Carefully place each pepper on a plate; spoon extra filling and sauce on top of pepper and sprinkle with pine nuts and parsley.

Per serving: 427 calories, 10 g fiber, 11 g protein, 4.8 g iron, 2.7 g zinc, 78 mg calcium, 0 mcg vitamin B12, 0 IU vitamin D, 115 g choline, .03 g omega 3s

COCONUT SPINACH CHICKPEAS

This Indian-inspired meal is the right temperature for spice lovers and haters—you can adjust the seasonings to make it as hot or not-hot as you'd like. Forget about cereal as your go-to dinner-in-a-pinch. This recipe relies on canned and frozen kitchen staples that you can easily keep on hand for nights when everyone else is having lamb chops.

Makes 4 servings

2 tablespoons canola oil

1 small onion, chopped

2 cloves garlic, crushed and minced

1 teaspoon curry powder

¼ teaspoon red pepper flakes (add more or less depending on how spicy you like it)

1 (14-ounce) can diced tomatoes, drained

1 (1-pound) bag frozen chopped spinach, defrosted and drained

1 (15-ounce) can chickpeas, drained and rinsed

1 cup canned lite coconut milk

½ teaspoon salt

In a medium saucepan, heat the oil over a medium flame. Sauté the onion until translucent. Add the garlic, curry powder, and red pepper flakes, and sauté for 1 minute. Mix in the diced tomatoes and cook for 3 to 5 minutes, or until hot. Add the spinach, chickpeas, coconut milk, and salt and bring to a simmer. Reduce heat and cook for about 10 minutes.

Serve with brown rice or another grain like quinoa.

Per serving: 376 calories, 10 g fiber, 13 g protein, 5.6 g iron, 1.4 g zinc, 202 mg calcium, 0 mcg vitamin B12, 0 IU vitamin D, 47 g choline, .64 g omega 3s

---

Dear Veggie,

Is it OK to try out being a vegetarian or vegan, and cheat sometimes?

Sincerely,
Uncommitted

~~~~~~

Dear Uncommitted,

Absolutely. You are not giving up meat (and possibly more) because you have a severe allergy to it (thank goodness—serious food allergies stink). You are choosing not to eat it because of moral, ethical, taste, or other reasons. And those reasons aren't as black and white as a life-threatening health condition. You have every right to change your diet, tweak it further, adjust it some more, and edit it for good measure. It's your life and your food.

You go girl,
VEGGIE

TOTALLY AMAZING VEG TACOS

Since everybody will assemble these tacos themselves at the table, your dining companions can easily pop out our black bean protein of choice for a meatier one like ground beef or chopped chicken. Of course, they may not want to when they see how delicious your meal looks.

MAKES 4 SERVINGS

3 tablespoons canola oil

1 small head broccoli, chopped into small florets

1 medium red pepper, diced (¼–½ inch cubes)

1 medium onion, diced (¼–½ inch cubes)

1 medium zucchini, diced (¼–½ inch cubes)

1 teaspoon garlic powder

½ teaspoon cumin

½ teaspoon chili powder

½ teaspoon salt

1 ripe avocado

2 medium plum tomatoes, chopped

1 (15-ounce) can black beans

¼ cup barbecue sauce

8 corn taco shells, hard or soft

Preheat oven to 475°F. Toss the oil, chopped broccoli, red pepper, onion, zucchini, garlic powder, cumin, chili powder, and salt in a medium roasting pan or cast iron pan. Roast the vegetables, tossing every 5 minutes, until well done—about 30 to 40 minutes. In the meantime, chop the avocado and tomato, mix together in a bowl to make a simple salsa, and set aside. In a small saucepan, heat the black beans and barbecue sauce over a low flame. Serve tacos "make your own" style—each person gets 2 taco shells, a scoop of veggies, a scoop of beans, and some avocado-tomato salsa.

Can serve with additional toppings: shredded cheese, sour cream, prepared guacamole, store-bought salsa, meat-based protein.

Per serving: 478 calories, 17 g fiber, 15 g protein, 4.4 g iron, 2.2 g zinc, 162 mg calcium, 0 mcg vitamin B12, 0 IU vitamin D, 52 g choline, 1.1 g omega 3s

LOADED BAKED POTATO BAR

With the right toppings, a simple baked potato can become a filling meal before your very eyes. And the nice thing about a DIY baked potato bar is that everyone gets to customize dinner to their liking. Use these guidelines to create a baked potato bar for your family, and get as creative as you'd like with the toppings and combos.

Makes 4 servings

4 large baking potatoes like Idaho or Russet

TOPPING IDEAS:
Frozen or fresh broccoli, steamed or sautéed
Frozen or fresh cauliflower, steamed or sautéed
Sautéed mushrooms and onions

1 can baked beans, heated (a very British way to serve your baked potato!)

Shredded cheese of your choice (examples: cheddar, Monterey Jack, feta, or parmesan)

Vegetarian or non-veg chili

Sour cream or Greek yogurt

Fresh herbs: chives, basil, cilantro, dill

Fake bacon bits

Guacamole

Salsa

Preheat oven to 400°F. Scrub the potatoes under running water. With a fork, poke a few holes in each potato. Wrap each one in aluminum foil, and place on a baking tray. Bake for about 50 to 60 minutes, or until soft. In the meantime, prepare your toppings and place with spoons in bowls on the counter or table so everyone can partake in the potato bar. Invite your friends or family to be creative and make a potato their way.

VEGHEAD BURGER

There are some great frozen veggie burgers to choose from in most grocery stores around the country. But it can still be fun to make your own. Try these scrumptious ones—you can share them with your fam or freeze them and toss on the grill when they're having a more conventional barbecue.

MAKES 8 BURGERS

207

1 (15-ounce) can lentils, drained and rinsed

½ teaspoon salt

2 cups white button mushrooms

1 small onion, chopped

2 cups cooked brown rice

1 cup rolled oats

2 tablespoons barbecue sauce

Preheat oven to 425°F. Put the lentils and salt in food processor and pulse until smooth. Place the lentil paste in a bowl. Add the mushrooms to food processor and pulse until chopped. In a medium saucepan, heat the oil. Add the onion and sauté until translucent. Add the mushrooms and cook until liquid evaporates, about 7 minutes. Transfer the mixture into bowl with lentil paste, add rice, oats, and barbecue sauce and mix well. Using your hands, form mixture into 8 evenly sized patties. Bake on a cookie sheet until browned, about 10 minutes on each side. Serve on hamburger buns with your favorite toppings.

Top Toppings

How you choose to dress your burger can turn each meal into something completely different. Try these combos to mix things up:

- The Traditionalist: American cheese, tomato, lettuce, sliced pickle
- The Californian: sliced avocado, tahini, alfalfa sprouts
- The Buon Appetito: mozzarella cheese and marinara sauce
- The South of the Border: guacamole and salsa
- The Spicy Rooster: sriracha sauce (hot sauce, often sold in a container with a rooster on it), shredded carrots, and fresh cilantro

Per serving: 205 calories, 8 g fiber, 10 g protein, 3 g iron, 1.9 g zinc, 29 mg calcium, 0 mcg vitamin B12, 2 IU vitamin D, 27 g choline, 0 g omega 3s

PROTEIN-PACKED PARMIGIANA

For as long as I can remember, one of my favorite foods on the planet has been eggplant parmigiana. And I used to think it was a pretty healthy choice—vegetables in tomato sauce! But once I started thinking more about health, I realized that my comfort food fave was severely lacking in the nutrition department. Sure, eggplant is a super healthy vegetable—but it sucks up oil like a sponge. And unlike chicken or veal parmigiana, the vegetarian version of the dish provides little protein to fill you up with (the cheese on top has some, but it's also loaded with heart-unhealthy saturated fat, so you don't want to eat too much). For a change, I've learned to make my parmigiana with tofu as the base. Tofu on its own is bland—but breaded and topped with sauce and cheese, it's pretty darn delish. And nutrition-wise, it's tops (especially if you use a nutrient-fortified tofu like I've recommended here). I've also added in an extra ingredient to add some color, texture, and nutrients. It's nothing like my local Italian restaurant used to make…but I'll eat my version any day (added bonus: I don't even feel like I need to take a nap after I eat it!)!

MAKES 4 SERVINGS

1 (14-ounce) package of Nasoya extra firm tofu plus, drained
¾ cup panko breadcrumbs*

1 ½ teaspoons dried oregano

¼ teaspoon pepper

2 tablespoons + 1 teaspoon olive oil

3 cups baby spinach

¾ cup tomato sauce

½ cup shredded mozzarella cheese

An hour before you are ready to cook, place the block of drained tofu in the freezer. Preheat oven to 400°F. Mix the panko, oregano, and pepper together in a bowl. Slice the frozen tofu the short way into 12 slabs (about ¼ inch thick). Dip each slice into a bowl of cool water and then into the panko mixture, coating both sides, using your hands to help the panko stick. Heat 2 tablespoons of oil in large skillet and pan fry tofu on one side until browned, flip and brown on the other side (add more oil if it's needed to keep bottom of pan slick). Coat bottom of 8" x 8" baking dish with ½ cup of tomato sauce and layer tofu slices. In the same skillet, add remaining one teaspoon of oil and sauté the spinach until wilted. Spread on top of the tofu slices. Top with the remaining sauce and mozzarella cheese. Bake until cheese is lightly browned, about 15 minutes.

Veganize it: Omit cheese, or use vegan cheese alternative.
★To make it gluten free, use gluten-free panko

Per serving: 337 calories, 4 g fiber, 20 g protein, 4.7 g iron, 1.1 g zinc, 534 mg calcium, 1.5 mcg vitamin B12, 134 IU vitamin D, 8 g choline, 0 g omega 3s

NO COMPROMISE SESAME NOODLES

This meal is easily customized for every member of your family—pop in chicken as the protein for meat eaters, tofu for the vegetarians. Oh, and it happens to be scrumptious, regardless of what you put on top of it.

MAKES 4 SERVINGS

1 (8-ounce) box thin pasta (you can use rice noodles, buckwheat noodles, or angel hair)★

¼ cup tamari★ + up to 4 teaspoons tamari, divided

¼ cup toasted sesame oil + up to 4 teaspoons sesame oil, divided

2 tablespoons maple syrup

1 clove garlic, minced

Red pepper flakes, to taste

1 (12-ounce) bag frozen broccoli

For each person eating tofu: ¼ (14-ounce) block of extra firm tofu per person, chopped into cubes

For each person eating chicken: 1 (4-ounce) chicken breast, chopped into cubes

4 scallions, chopped

¼ cup sesame seeds

Prepare the pasta according to package directions. In the meantime, in a medium bowl whisk together the tamari, sesame oil, maple syrup, garlic, and red pepper flakes. Defrost the frozen broccoli in a microwave or on the stovetop. In two skillets, prepare your proteins: heat 1 teaspoon of sesame oil and 1 teaspoon of tamari per serving of protein, add the tofu or chicken and stir fry (tofu: until lightly browned; chicken: until pieces are cooked through). When pasta is ready, toss with tamari mixture and broccoli. Distribute the noodles and broccoli into bowls and "pop in" your protein options. Sprinkle each bowl with scallions and sesame seeds.

*To make it gluten free, use rice noodles or another gluten-free noodle, and wheat-free tamari.

Per serving (using angel hair and tofu): 454 calories, 6 g fiber, 21 g protein, 5.2 g iron, 1.9 g zinc, 208 mg calcium, 0 mcg vitamin B12, 2 IU vitamin D, 21 g choline, 0 g omega 3s

SO NOT REALLY SAUSAGE AND PEPPERS

This hearty dinner is a favorite among meat lovers. But replace meat-based sausages with veggie ones (I love, love, love the ones by The Original Field Roast Grain Meat Company, but there are lots of others to try that you may like better) and you'll have a super filling dinner for all.

MAKES 4 SERVINGS

2 tablespoons + 2 tablespoons olive oil
4 vegetarian sausage links, sliced into rounds*
1/8 teaspoon red pepper flakes (more or less to taste)
2 large onions, sliced
1 large red bell pepper, sliced

1 large green bell pepper, sliced

2 cups tomato sauce

In a medium pan, heat 2 tablespoons of olive oil on medium heat. Add the sausage slices, and sauté until lightly browned on both sides. Remove from pan. Add the remaining olive oil, red pepper flakes, onion, red and green pepper, and sauté until soft, about 10–15 minutes. Add the tomato sauce, and bring to a simmer. Add the sausage to mixture and serve with pasta, rice, or as a sandwich on Italian bread.

*To make it gluten free, be sure to use gluten-free veggie sausage (many are not).

Per serving: 294 calories, 6 g fiber, 9 g protein, 3.6 g iron, .65 g zinc, 65 mg calcium, 0 mcg vitamin B12, 0 IU vitamin D, 27 g choline, 0 g omega 3s

GRACE'S NOT-GGETS

When I interviewed my panel of teenage vegetarians for this book, I asked them what meat-containing food they most missed. One of my panelists named Grace had so much to say about chicken nuggets that I just had to see what I could do. These tofu-based nuggets are not chicken, no doubt about that. But they're savory, crunchy, and oh-so-dippable—I do hope that they help Grace scratch that chicken nugget itch she's been having!

MAKES 4 SERVINGS

1 (14-ounce) block extra firm tofu
1 egg
½ cup panko breadcrumbs
1 tablespoon ground flaxseeds
3 tablespoons canola oil

Slice the tofu into 8 ½-inch slices and then in half (should make 16 pieces). Place the tofu in a bowl and cover with boiling water. Allow to sit for 15 minutes. In a medium bowl, whisk the egg. Place the breadcrumbs on a plate and toss with flaxseeds. Drain water from tofu. Dip each piece in egg and roll in breadcrumb mixture until coated. In a medium saucepan, heat 2 tablespoons of oil over medium heat. Pan fry each nugget on both sides until browned. Add more oil as needed. Serve with your favorite dipping sauce (ketchup, mustard, barbecue sauce, etc.), and a side of vegetables, of course!

Veganize it: Instead of dipping the tofu in egg, use water and your hands to make the breadcrumbs stick to the tofu.

Per serving: 193 calories, 1 g fiber, 10 g protein, 1.7 g iron, .9 g zinc, 50 mg calcium, .15 mcg vitamin B12, 13 IU vitamin D, 41 g choline, .97 g omega 3s

Dear Veggie,

I am going to dinner at my friend's house and her mom wants to make something special for me because everyone else is having steak. I don't want her to have to go out of her way for me to make something else. What should I do?

From,
Insecure about Imposing

Dear Insecure,

Go easy on yourself! Your friend's mom doesn't "have to" go out of her way for you, as you put it. Rather, she wants to. How nice! If a person offers to accommodate your dietary preferences, there's nothing wrong with graciously accepting her offer. What you can do is make sure your friend's mom knows just how much you appreciate her thoughtfulness—thank her genuinely, and ask if there's anything you can do to help prepare your part of the meal. And most definitely help clear the table after dinner's over, and maybe even offer to do some of the dishes. The best way to not impose on a considerate host is to be a good guest.

Thank you for your question, Insecure. I really, truly appreciate it. Now, can I help you clear the table?
VEGGIE

SCRUMPTIOUS SNACKS, SIDES, AND DESSERTS

CRUNCHY CHICKPEA MUNCHIES

This addictive snack is packed with protein, which means it's a great way to power up and keep you energized during soccer practice or a long study session.

MAKES 4 SERVINGS

1 (12-ounce) can chickpeas, drained
2 tablespoons canola oil
Spices to taste: my favorites are smoked chipotle and pimentón, but you can try anything—garlic and onion powders, even sweet spices like cinnamon and nutmeg
Salt and pepper to taste

Preheat oven to 425°F. Pat the chickpeas dry with paper towels. Toss with the olive oil, spices, salt, and pepper. Spread onto cookie sheet and bake until browned and crispy, tossing every 5 to 10 minutes, for about 30 minutes.

Per serving: 163 calories, 4 g fiber, 4 g protein, 1.1 g iron, .9 g zinc, 27 mg calcium, 0 mcg vitamin B12, 2 IU vitamin D, 28 g choline, .64 g omega 3s

CHOOSE YOUR OWN ADVENTURE POPCORN

Popcorn is one of the best snack foods ever. It's fun and delicious to eat, and it's also healthy—depending on what you put on it. Instead of getting it at the movie theater (ick—what exactly is "buttery topping," anyway?) or out of a microwave pack (some of the ingredients in those can be pretty gross too), make it in an air popper or on the stovetop (see below for directions). Drizzle on some oil (like olive or flax) and then dress it up however your little heart desires. Here are some toppings worth considering:

SPICY:
Chili powder
Ginger powder
Ground chipotle powder
Pimentón

SAVORY:
Grated parmesan cheese
Oregano
Parsley
Rosemary
Thyme
Nutritional yeast

SWEET:
Chocolate chips
Cinnamon
Hot chocolate mix
Mini M&Ms
Powdered sugar

DIY Stovetop Popcorn

Once you see how easy and delicious it is to pop popcorn on the stove, you'll wonder why you ever made it in the microwave. Follow these simple steps to the perfect snack:

1. Heat three tablespoons of oil (peanut, canola, and coconut all work well) on medium-high heat in a medium pot with a lid.
2. When the oil is hot, add 1/3 cup popcorn kernels.
3. As the kernels begin to pop, shake the pot gently so the unpopped kernels sink to the bottom.
4. Once popping slows to once every 3 to 4 seconds, turn heat off and pour popcorn into a bowl. Add your favorite fancy seasonings—though a simple sprinkle of salt works great too.

KRAZY KALE CHIPS

Krazy with a K because that's what people may think you are for eating something called "kale chips." But hear me out. It's not like you need a vegetarian replacement for potato chips or anything, I know that. It just turns out that kale chips are really, really good. Really good! They're also addictive. And with bone-building calcium and vitamin K, as well as other important nutrients, kale is a super smart food to find its way into any teenage girl's diet.

Makes 4 servings

1 medium bunch kale, washed, dried, and chopped into 1- to 2-inch pieces

1 tablespoon olive oil
Kosher or sea salt

Preheat oven to 300°F. Toss the kale with olive oil and place in one layer onto baking sheet. Bake until crisp, tossing every 5 minutes, for about 15 to 20 minutes. Sprinkle with salt. Add additional seasonings like nutritional yeast, chili powder, and ground chipotle as desired. Taste best when eaten with your fingers!

Per serving: 63 calories, 1 g fiber, 2 g protein, 1.2 g iron, .3 g zinc, 91 mg calcium, 0 mcg vitamin B12, 2 IU vitamin D, 0 g choline, 0 g omega 3s

SUPER SWEET POTATO "FRIES"

Who doesn't love french fries? These ones, made with über-nutritious sweet potatoes, taste delish and have the bonus of being really good for you too. They make a perfect accompaniment to your favorite veggie burger, sandwich, or meat-free nuggets.

MAKES 4 SERVINGS

3 medium sweet potatoes, scrubbed
3 tablespoons canola oil
1 tablespoon cornstarch
¼ teaspoon garlic powder
¼ teaspoon salt

Preheat oven to 425°F. Slice the sweet potatoes into ¼-inch thick slabs, and then again into ¼-inch sticks that resemble french fries. Toss with the canola oil and cornstarch, until evenly coated. Spread in a single layer on a baking sheet and sprinkle with garlic powder and salt. Bake until well done, about 45 minutes, tossing every 10 minutes. Serve with ketchup or your favorite dipping sauce.

Per serving: 300 calories, 3 g fiber, 2 g protein, .8 g iron, .3 g zinc, 30 mg calcium, 0 mcg vitamin B12, 2 IU vitamin D, 12 g choline, .23 g omega 3s

CHOCOLATE POWER MOUSSE

Craving a rich, delicious dessert? This one will hit the spot—and your friends will be amazed to hear it's vegan.

MAKES 6 SERVINGS

1 ½ cups dark chocolate chips
½ cup vanilla-flavored coconut milk
1 pound silken tofu
1 pinch salt

In a small saucepan, whisk the chocolate chips and coconut milk together over low heat until completely combined (no lumps!). Pour into food processor with tofu and salt. Pulse until smooth. Spoon into 6 small dessert bowls and chill in the refrigerator until firm (about 30 minutes). If you want to be fancy, layer it with banana and strawberry slices in a glass cup for a pudding parfait.

Per serving: 357 calories, 6 g fiber, 12 g protein, 3.2 g iron, .6 g zinc, 73 mg calcium, 0 mcg vitamin B12, 0 IU vitamin D, 0 g choline, 0 g omega 3s

---

Dear Veggie,

I love meat. But my best friend doesn't. Actually, she's decided to stop eating it altogether. I'm worried about our friendship. Do I have to be a vegetarian when I'm around her now? Will she be offended if I eat a cheeseburger in front of her?

Sincerely,
A Good Friend

~~~~~~

Dear Friend,

Forget about being a good friend, I'm nominating you for Friend of the Year. It is super caring and supportive of you to take your BFFs feelings into consideration like this. The answer is ultimately going to depend on your friend. The most important thing you can do is ask her how she feels. I do think that in general most vegetarians don't care about what other people eat in front of them—as long as those people don't give them a hard time about their choices! My guess is that as long as you keep on being such a great friend, your BFF will be considerate of your preferences as you have been kind about hers.

In friendship,
VEGGIE

BANANA JOE'S ICE CREAM

I discovered this ice cream in Hawaii, where bananas grow pretty much everywhere, at a fruit stand called "Banana Joe." Once I got home, I got in the habit of making my own Banana Joe ice cream. I buy lots of bananas at a time, peel them, wrap in aluminum foil, and freeze, just so they're ready to be turned into a luscious, creamy dessert when the craving hits. If you really love this recipe, you can save up for the same machine that they use in Hawaii—it's called a Champion Juicer, and it's perfect for turning frozen fruit into healthy ice cream (beware, it's pretty pricey). But you can also make it in a regular old food processor that almost everyone has in their kitchen.

Makes 1 serving

One frozen banana

Break the banana into pieces. Put in food processor and pulse until pieces are broken down as much as possible. With a rubber spatula, push banana pieces back to center of food processor. Repeat this as many times as you need to until banana reaches ice cream consistency. You can also add in additional ingredients like peanut butter, chocolate chips, or cocoa powder to add an extra flavor to your banana "ice cream." Use rubber spatula to remove from food processor.

You can enjoy this banana "ice cream" on its own or with any favorite topping. Here are some worth trying out:

Shredded coconut

Toasted walnuts

Chocolate chips

Granola

Sliced strawberries

Per serving: 105 calories, 3 g fiber, 1 g protein, .3 g iron, .2 g zinc, 6 mg calcium, 0 mcg vitamin B12, 0 IU vitamin D, 12 g choline, 0 g omega 3s

CHIA POWER PUDDING

It's simple to turn these super-healthy seeds (available at stores like Whole Foods, Trader Joe's, and Walmart) into a delish pudding. You see, chia seeds absorb a ton of liquid, which turns them sort of gelatinous—if you like tapioca, you'll like this. What's more, they're packed with the plant-based form of omega-3 fatty acids, which means they're good for your heart, brain, skin, and more.

MAKES 1 SERVING

½ cup vanilla coconut milk

2 tablespoons chia seeds

1 teaspoon maple syrup

1 pinch salt

Mix ingredients together in a small bowl. Whisk once every 5 minutes for 15 minutes so seeds begin to absorb liquid evenly.

Cover and refrigerate overnight, or at least 5 hours. Serve plain or with fruit.

Per serving: 236 calories, 11 g fiber, 5 g protein, 2.4 g iron, 1.3 g zinc, 349 mg calcium, 0 mcg vitamin B12, 2 IU vitamin D, .3 g choline, 5.05 g omega 3s

• ACKNOWLEDGMENTS •

This book would not be here if it wasn't for the hard work, dedication, and love of many people.

Danielle Chiotti and her team at Upstart Crow Literary for believing in this project and my ability to pull it off. Her advice, creativity, and words of encouragement have helped tremendously at every step in the process and made it all just so much fun.

Leah Hultenschmidt and everyone at Sourcebooks for taking a chance on a first-time author and helping take this book from an idea into a valuable resource for "smart girls" everywhere.

The vegetarian and veg-curious teenagers I interviewed whose stories helped enliven these pages: Sajada Bhuiyan, Brianna Cunneen, Nicole Fegan, Jill Golub, Tori Grant, Alicia Kerr, Alex Lasser-Gold, Sarah Mackenzie, Sophie Martel, Jessie Meyers, Rachel Newman, Jenna Pasternak, Vivian Ponte-Fritz, Jordyn Ramelli, Andie Shapiro, Alexandra Soscia, Grace Taylor, Sarah Taylor, Stephanie Tock, and Krithi Vachaspati.

All of the friends and family who shared stories, brainstormed titles, and jumped up and down when I told them this idea was becoming a real book. A very special thanks to my lovelies who volunteered their professional expertise: Teresa Dumain, Terra Fuhr, Larissa McKenna, and Cynthia Sass. How lucky I am to have them all in my life.

My parents Janet and Michael, who nurtured my love for

writing and books, backed me 100 percent when I first experi- mented with going veg, and taught me by example to pursue a career I am engaged in and passionate about. I adore them both, and forgive them for the couches. Sort of.

Scott, a vegetarian by marriage, who has the courage of my convictions. He simultaneously plays the roles of daydream catcher, sounding board, editor, taste tester, and BFF, and makes me a way better person than I was when he found me.

And finally, to Liliana, whose impending arrival helped me meet the biggest deadline of my life (and kept it in perspective, as I had a far bigger one around the corner), and whose bright eyes remind me every day why I wanted to write a book like this. May she—and all young girls—always feel empowered by her decisions (edible and otherwise), and have the support and tools she needs to thrive.

•ABOUT THE AUTHOR•

Rachel Meltzer Warren, MS, RDN, is a former twelve-year-old vegetarian who grew up to be a nutrition writer, educator, and counselor. She spends her time in and around NYC, where she specializes in helping kids, teens, and parents cultivate a taste for healthful food.